BayAreaNewsGroup
San Jose Mercury News • Contra Costa Times • Oakland Tribune

COMEBACK
KINGS

THE SAN FRANCISCO GIANTS' INCREDIBLE
2012 CHAMPIONSHIP SEASON

WORLD SERIES CHAMPIONS

Giants closer Sergio Romo, who collected saves in the final three World Series games, embraces catcher Buster Posey. Their Giants teammates run out to celebrate San Francisco's second title in three years. (Karl Mondon/Staff)

Copyright © 2012 by Bay Area News Group
No part of this publication may be reproduced, stored in a retrieval system, or transmitted in any form
by any means, electronic, mechanical, photocopying, or otherwise, without prior written permission of the
publisher, Triumph Books LLC, 814 North Franklin Street; Chicago, Illinois 60610.

This book is book is available in quantity at special discounts for your group or organization.
For further information, contact:

Triumph Books LLC
814 North Franklin Street
Chicago, Illinois 60610
Phone: (312) 337-0747
www.triumphbooks.com

Printed in U.S.A.
ISBN: 978-1-60078-750-8

Bay Area News Group
Mac Tully, Publisher and President, Bay Area News Group
David J. Butler, Editor and Vice President for News, MediaNewsGroup
Bert Robinson, Managing Editor, Bay Area News Group
Bud Geracie, Executive Sports Editor, Bay Area News Group

Content packaged by Mojo Media, Inc.
Joe Funk: Editor
Jason Hinman: Creative Director

Front cover photo by Gary Reyes/Staff. Back cover photos by Nhat V. Meyer/Staff.

Giants right fielder Hunter Pence, who delivered fiery speeches all postseason long, rallies the troops before Game 5 of the NLDS. (Getty Images)

CONTENTS

INTRODUCTION
By Alex Pavlovic

The band of misfits gave way to a band of brothers, driven by the simple desire to spend one more day playing the game, one more day together on the diamond. On their final day as a team — and surely it will be the last as no team, however great, returns the next spring fully intact — the 2012 San Francisco Giants paraded down Market Street with a World Series trophy for the second time in three years.

The short trip down Market capped a long, improbable journey, one that seemed at its end numerous times between April and October.

During their stunning run, the Giants, a team with a heavy Latin presence, embraced the Spanish word "pelea," meaning "fight."

"We fight like an upside-down cat," leadoff hitter Angel Pagan said.

As it turned out, they had nearly as many lives, too.

The Giants could have folded in April when closer Brian Wilson was lost for the year, or in mid-August when All-Star left fielder Melky Cabrera was suspended, or a week later when the Dodgers swung a set of blockbuster trades in an attempt to deliver the knockout blow. Instead, the Giants ran away with the division.

They could have surrendered in October when twice they found themselves one loss from elimination. Instead, sparked by a fiery Hunter Pence speech, they pushed their chips to the center of the table. If they were going to go down, they were going to go down fighting.

Pelea!

"These guys come out with their slingshots and rocks and they're going to fight you," third base coach Tim Flannery said. "These guys just believe."

The Giants believed when they fell behind two games to none in the National League Division Series before stunning the Cincinnati Reds by winning three straight games on the banks of the Ohio River. They believed when they fell behind three games to one in the National League Championship Series, only to outscore the St. Louis Cardinals 20-1 over the next three games.

In the World Series, the Giants were brimming with belief.

They beat Tigers ace Justin Verlander in Game 1 and beat him badly, Pablo Sandoval leading the way with a historic three-homer night. They won the next two games by not allowing a run, the first back-to-back Series shutouts since the legendary Baltimore Orioles staff blanked the Dodgers three straight in 1966. They completed the sweep with a 4-3 victory that was absurdly emblematic of their season, fighting back from a deficit to win on a 10th-inning single by Marco Scutaro,

Giants center fielder Angel Pagan congratulates Ryan Theriot. In the starting lineup as the designated hitter, Theriot scored the winning run in Game 4 of the World Series. (Gary Reyes/Staff)

"Look into each other's eyes, I want one more day with you. We must not give in. We owe it to each other. Play for each other!" — **Right fielder Hunter Pence**

the journeyman infielder who became a giant star after his July 27 acquisition.

The Giants had every answer against Detroit, just as they had an answer to every challenge that arose along the way.

"Everyone counted us out four or five times," pitcher Ryan Vogelsong said. "I think it's the perseverance through the whole season that's where we draw the confidence that it's not over until the last out is made."

Their mettle was tested the first week of the season when Wilson, the man who clinched the final out of the 2010 World Series, needed reconstructive elbow surgery for a second time. The entire bullpen, led by charismatic right-hander Sergio Romo, picked up the slack.

In all, the Giants made 18 trips to the disabled list, two by Sandoval, who missed 53 games with first a hand injury and then a hamstring strain. Looking for a temporary solution at third base, General Manager Brian Sabean made a trade that barely registered on the national radar, sending minor league infielder Charlie Culberson to Colorado for Scutaro. The deal came to be known as a "blockbuster," as did Scutaro, who earned that nickname while leading the team's late charge into the autumn. In October, he also became forever known as MVP of the National League Championship Series.

The Giants could have been excused for packing it in when Cabrera was suspended, for looking back on their series of misfortunes and determining that it just wasn't their year. Manager Bruce Bochy had a different idea: "Focus forward," he told his players, and they did.

Needing to win an unprecedented three straight road games in the LDS against Cincinnati, Bochy delivered another speech before Game 3. Then Pence stood up in the cramped visitors' clubhouse and started bouncing around like a linebacker.

"Look into each other's eyes," Pence screamed. "I want one more day with you. We must not give in. We owe it to each other. Play for each other!"

The Giants came out of the "rally throng" (as it was termed by our Daniel Brown) and toppled the Reds, then stunned the Cardinals, becoming the first team in MLB history to reach a World Series by winning six elimination games. The Tigers proved to be no match.

Posey, coming off the gruesome home plate collision that ended his 2011 season and threatened his career, punctuated one of the best seasons ever by a catcher with a grand slam that downed the Reds. Barry Zito, the long-beleaguered pitcher so out of sync in 2010 that the Giants left him off the postseason roster, won two of the biggest games in franchise history with dominating performances. Tim Lincecum shook off an unimaginably rocky season to become a shutdown reliever in October.

By the time the Giants were done throwing haymakers, their hands were being fitted for championship rings. ∎

Giants pitcher Matt Cain, who allowed three runs during his Game 4 start in the World Series, celebrates the final out of the seventh inning. (Nhat V. Meyer/Staff)

WORLD SERIES: GAME 1
OCTOBER 24, 2012 | GIANTS 8, TIGERS 3

Pablo's Show
Zito Solid, Sandoval Hits Three Home Runs in Game 1 Rout
By Alex Pavlovic

> **"(Sandoval) had one of those unbelievable World Series nights that they'll be talking about for years. I tip my hat to him."**
>
> — **Tigers manager Jim Leyland**

SAN FRANCISCO—After winning six elimination games to reach the World Series, the Giants said they wanted to take an easier route this time around. They got off to a crushing start Wednesday, making it look easy against the best pitcher in baseball.

Pablo Sandoval homered in his first three at-bats and Barry Zito was dominant again as the Giants cruised past Justin Verlander and the Detroit Tigers 8-3 in the first game of the World Series.

Sandoval hit two homers off Verlander, and in his third at-bat he took Al Alburquerque deep to join one of the most elite lists in sports. He's the fourth player in MLB history to hit three home runs in a World Series game, along with Hall of Famers Babe Ruth (who did it twice) and Reggie Jackson and future Hall of Famer Albert Pujols. Appropriately, the bat Sandoval used to hit the first two homers — it broke in his third plate appearance — was donated to the Hall of Fame.

"I still can't believe it," Sandoval said. "I don't try to hit home runs. I'm not trying to do too much right now, especially at this time of the season."

Sandoval did plenty, and he did it on a stage that had previously represented the low point of his career. Out of shape and out of sync, Sandoval had just three at-bats and played in one game in the 2010 World Series. That was much more action than the Giants gave Zito, who was left off the roster altogether.

On Wednesday, the redemption train rolled right through the Tigers.

Verlander, the reigning American League MVP and Cy Young Award winner, had given up just two runs in his first three postseason starts. Sandoval and the Giants doubled that number in the first three innings. With two outs in

During the first inning, Giants third baseman Pablo Sandoval hits the first of his three Game 1 home runs. He is the fourth player in major league history to blast three homers in one World Series game. (Karl Mondon/Staff)

"I still can't believe it. I don't try to hit home runs. I'm not trying to do too much right now, especially at this time of the season." — Third baseman Pablo Sandoval

the first, Sandoval crushed an elevated 95 mph fastball over the center field wall, becoming just the sixth player to homer on an 0-2 pitch from Verlander.

"We've seen a lot of stuff from Pablo," Zito said. "It's kind of hard to impress us with what we've seen, but we were all very impressed tonight."

Others in a dugout that celebrated with group dancing and sunflower seed showers used different words.

"We were all kind of shocked," Brandon Crawford said.

"He hit that ball to dead center — that's the most amazing thing," Aubrey Huff said. "You're taking a ball to center against a pitcher that's the best on the planet. It was a great pitch, too.

"We were looking at it on the (scoreboard) and going, 'How did he hit that? How?' I don't know who hits that ball, maybe just Barry Bonds in his prime. It was astonishing."

The stunning show was only just beginning.

The Giants had another two-out rally in the third, and it started with a play that confirmed any suspicions one might have that something special is at work at AT&T Park. Angel Pagan hit a grounder to third that bounced off the bag and ricocheted into left field for a double. Marco Scutaro followed with a single to center, scoring Pagan.

"I think we've kind of earned those breaks," Crawford said, smiling. "We had some balls early in the playoffs that didn't go our way."

Everything went the Giants' way on this night. Sandoval stunned Verlander again a batter later, lining another 95 mph fastball into the seats, this time in left field. Verlander, who had allowed only one multi-homer game all season, stood on the mound and muttered, 'Wow,' before turning to the Tigers dugout, frowning and shaking his head.

"It was unbelievable," Tigers manager Jim Leyland said. "This guy had one of those unbelievable World Series nights that they'll be talking about for years. I tip my hat to him."

With his second blast, Sandoval became the first player since Andruw Jones in 1996 to hit two homers in the first three innings of a World Series game. He wasn't done, but first Zito would add a historic footnote of his own.

Zito added to Verlander's pain in the fourth with a two-out RBI single to left on a 97 mph fastball. Zito, a .097 career hitter, has an RBI in his last two starts, helping make the Giants the first team in MLB history to get an RBI from the starting pitcher in four straight postseason games.

"Yeah, Zito is more surprised than anybody," said Tim Lincecum, who later relieved Zito.

Sandoval padded his historic night in the fifth, hitting an Alburquerque pitch out to center. He made some AT&T Park history, too. The only previous three-homer game at AT&T Park came when the Los Angeles Dodgers' Kevin Elster did it on April 11, 2000.

That was the very first regular-season game on the shores of McCovey Cove.

Zito earned a Game 1 start with a brilliant outing in Game 5 of the N.L. Championship Series, and he was nearly as good Wednesday night. Zito limited the Tigers to one run on six hits over $5^2/_3$ innings, twice getting help with diving catches from left fielder Gregor Blanco.

The Giants tacked on two more runs in the seventh, with Sandoval contributing a scorched single to center. Sandoval fell short in his bid to become the first player in baseball history to homer four times in a World Series game, but that hardly mattered on this night.

Since falling behind 3-1 in the NLCS, the Giants have won four straight, outscoring opponents 28-4.

"We're having fun right now," Sandoval said. "When you get that mindset, everything goes your way." ∎

Giants third baseman Pablo Sandoval circles the bases during the fifth inning after hitting his third home run in Game 1. (Gary Reyes/Staff)

WORLD SERIES: GAME 2

OCTOBER 25, 2012 | GIANTS 2, TIGERS 0

Rolling Their Way

Giants Blank Detroit Tigers, Hold Two-Game Edge

By Alex Pavlovic

> **These guys come out with their slingshots and rocks, and they're going to fight you. These guys just believe."**
>
> — Third base coach
> Tim Flannery

SAN FRANCISCO—After a series of hard-to-believe, game-changing plays, the Giants have learned to stop asking questions.

Hunter Pence's triple-double that turned in midair in Game 7 of the National League Championship Series was soon followed by Angel Pagan's rally-igniting double off third base in Game 1 of the World Series. In Thursday's 2-0 Game 2 win over the Detroit Tigers, the Giants scored the winning run in large part because of a Gregor Blanco bunt that died on the third base line and loaded the bases.

"It's been going our way lately," shortstop Brandon Crawford said. "It's kind of nice that it's happening to us at the right time. It's the baseball gods, I guess."

Crawford drove in the go-ahead run on a double-play grounder with the bases loaded in the seventh, a batter after Blanco's improbable bunt. It was the ultimate grind-it-out rally for what has become the ultimate grind-it-out team.

"These guys come out with their slingshots and rocks, and they're going to fight you," third base coach Tim Flannery said. "These guys just believe."

The Giants scored both their runs on outs, but some conventional rocks were thrown, too. Madison Bumgarner was superb through seven innings, and Santiago Casilla and Sergio Romo pitched perfect innings of relief. The trio held the Tigers to two hits, a World Series record for Giants pitchers.

After a 2-0 victory in a two-hitter, the Giants head to Detroit with a 2-0 series lead, just as they had in 2010. That year, they beat a former Cy Young winner (Cliff Lee) in Game 1 of the World Series and shut out the Texas Rangers in Game 2. The same path has been followed this season, after they victimized reigning

Giants pitcher Madison Bumgarner showed his postseason moxie, striking out eight Tigers hitters while throwing seven shutout innings for the Game 2 victory. (Nhat V. Meyer/Staff)

A.L. Cy Young winner Justin Verlander in Game 1.

"It feels the same, but we know it's not going to be the same until we win a World Series," left-hander Jeremy Affeldt said. "They're not going to roll over."

Against Bumgarner, the Tigers had little choice. Bumgarner gave up 10 combined runs in two previous starts this postseason — both of them losses — and briefly lost his spot in the rotation. But pitching coach Dave Righetti found and fixed a mechanical flaw in Bumgarner's motion, and Righetti and manager Bruce Bochy felt confident that Bumgarner could find his old form.

They were right.

Bumgarner struck out eight in seven shutout innings, giving up just two hits and walking two. In his tightest moment, he benefited from another stellar play from a defense that has sparkled in the postseason.

Prince Fielder was hit by a pitch to lead off the second inning, and Delmon Young followed with a double to left that caromed off the wall by the Giants bullpen. Tigers third base coach Gene Lamont sent Fielder, who is listed at 275 pounds, home as Blanco came up firing. He overthrew Crawford, the first cutoff man, but Marco Scutaro was in the perfect spot to grab the relay and made a perfect strike to Buster Posey at the plate.

"I don't know what Marco was doing there," Blanco said, laughing. "But he was there. It ended up being a great play."

Posey capped it with a swipe tag on Fielder inches before he crossed the plate. Instead of having two runners in scoring position with no outs, Bumgarner had an out and a roaring crowd behind him, and soon he was out of the inning.

"I think Gene just got a little overaggressive," Tigers coach Jim Leyland said.

The Giants felt there was a reason for the aggressive decision. After scoring just one run off Barry Zito, the Tigers were blanked by Bumgarner. Through two games,

the high-powered Tigers offense has just three runs.

"You can't ask from anything more from the starters," Romo said. "What a time to go out there with your best outings of the year. They talk about our starting rotation for a reason."

Bumgarner continued to show why he's a pitcher the Giants hope the rest of the league is talking about for years to come. In two career World Series starts, the 23-year-old Bumgarner hasn't given up a run and has allowed just five hits in 15 innings. Bumgarner's 15-inning scoreless streak in his first two postseason starts is the longest by a Giants pitcher since Hall of Famer Christy Mathewson did it 107 years ago.

"I definitely felt better," Bumgarner said. "I was able to make pitches. That's all you can do."

Bumgarner wasn't able to will the Giants to a lead, but Blanco and Crawford came through in the seventh. Pence hit a leadoff single, and Brandon Belt walked ahead of Blanco, who then put down a bunt he called "the best of my life."

The ball came to a rest 30 feet up the line, stunning the Tigers and Flannery, who has been working with Blanco on his bunting since the start of spring training. Flannery knows AT&T Park as well as anybody, and knows that a bunt down the dirt will always roll foul. This one didn't.

"It's a credit to Blanco to get a pitch he could put right down on the chalk," Flannery said, smiling.

Blanco said he was shocked when he looked back and saw that "I put it in the perfect spot."

A batter later the Giants had the lead on Crawford's grounder to second that scored Pence. Two innings later they had a 2-0 Series lead, one they're comfortable with. But after getting to the World Series with a pair of comeback series wins, the Giants to a man said they won't get too comfortable as they settle in for the flight to Detroit.

"You can't count Detroit out," Romo said. "Look at what we were able to do to get here." ■

During the seventh inning, Giants right fielder Hunter Pence scores the game's first run. It would be the only run San Francisco needed in the 2-0 win. (Nhat V. Meyer/Staff)

The Giants celebrate their Game 2 victory. After holding serve at home, they headed to Detroit up 2-0 in the series. (Jose Carlos Fajardo/Staff)

WORLD SERIES: GAME 3
OCTOBER 27, 2012 | GIANTS 2, TIGERS 0

Motor City Madness

Vogelsong, Lincecum Keep Tigers Quiet

By Alex Pavlovic

> **I've been waiting for this since I was 5 years old. I wasn't going down without a fight, that's for sure.**
>
> — Pitcher
> **Ryan Vogelsong**

DETROIT—You can learn everything you need to know about the Giants' dominance not by looking at the box score but at the interview podium after games. Major League Baseball has been selecting a steady stream of pitchers to represent the team, and Saturday the lights shone on not one, but two starting pitchers.

Ryan Vogelsong and Tim Lincecum sat side-by-side, so different, but in this 2-0 victory over the Detroit Tigers, so alike. Both were forceful on the mound, taking the bite out of a Tigers lineup that was shut out twice all season and now has been shut out in back-to-back World Series games.

The Giants are the first team since 1966 to pitch two consecutive World Series shutouts and, with a 3-0 series lead, are on the verge of a second championship in three years. Lincecum, a two-time Cy Young Award winner, and Vogelsong, a journeyman-turned-All-Star, differ in this arena. Vogelsong is desperate for the ring Lincecum already has.

"I've been waiting for this since I was 5 years old," Vogelsong said after his first World Series start. "I wasn't going to go down without a fight, that's for sure."

Vogelsong brought the fight to the Tigers, repeatedly stifling rallies and leaving after $5^2/_3$ scoreless innings. Vogelsong joined Hall of Famer Christy Mathewson as the only pitchers to throw at least five innings and give up no more than one run in each of their first four postseason starts.

Giants shortstop Brandon Crawford singles in the second inning to score Gregor Blanco, giving San Francisco a 2-0 lead it would not relinquish. (Nhat V. Meyer/Staff)

"
They've got to beat us four times in a row now. But after the comebacks we've had, anything is possible. We can't sleep on these guys." — Closer Sergio Romo

In 24²/₃ postseason innings, Vogelsong has allowed just three runs and 16 hits.

"He's that kind of guy that's just going to leave it out there on the field," Lincecum said. "He'll give you everything he's got, give you the shirt off his back if he has to."

Lincecum didn't need Vogelsong's jersey, but he did inherit one of his runners with the Giants leading 2-0 in the sixth. Lincecum got the Giants out of that inning and dominated for two more, getting the ball to closer Sergio Romo for a perfect ninth.

"Look at that job they did," Romo said, shaking his head. "They set the tempo. Here we are in the World Series just trying to complement each other."

Out of the bullpen, Lincecum has been the perfect complement for a rotation he once paced. In five relief appearances this postseason, he has given up one run and three hits in 13 innings, striking out 17.

"I'm just going to go out there as a safety net kind of thing," Lincecum said. "Just being able to contribute is the biggest thing for me. I know this season I didn't exactly do what I wanted to do, so to go out there and just be able to do something for the team, that's really my goal."

Through three World Series games, the Giants starters and Lincecum have given up just one run, but the dominance stretches further back. The Giants have won six straight and haven't trailed since they lost Game 4 of the NLCS to the St. Louis Cardinals.

The staff has pitched four shutouts in the past six games and given up just four runs. Over that same span, Giants pitchers have driven in four runs.

"The way they've been going, it seems like one or two runs is enough," shortstop Brandon Crawford said.

Crawford helped get Vogelsong an early lead. Gregor Blanco's second-inning triple scored Hunter Pence, and Crawford's single brought home Blanco to give Vogelsong a 2-0 cushion that would be more than enough.

Vogelsong got inning-ending double plays in the first and third innings but saved his greatest escape act for the fifth inning. After loading the bases with one out, Vogelsong struck out Quintin Berry and got Triple Crown winner Miguel Cabrera to pop up to short.

"I go with my gut, and Vogey goes with his gut," catcher Buster Posey said of the two fastballs to Cabrera. "If I put something down that he's not convicted about, he'll shake."

How often did Vogelsong shake off a Posey pitch selection Saturday night?

"Two or three times," Vogelsong said, smiling. "And some of those are planned. I trust him, and I think he takes a lot of what he does at the plate and uses it behind the plate. We were on the same page the whole game. Give him a lot of credit for what we've been doing."

With Posey handling a staff of aces and the defense — led by Crawford and Blanco — handling anything that doesn't find Posey's glove, the Giants are on the verge of another ticker-tape parade.

Twenty of the previous 23 teams to take a 3-0 lead in the World Series have ended up with a sweep. The other three teams won in five games.

"They've got to beat us four times in a row now," Romo said. "But after the comebacks we've had, we know anything is possible. We can't sleep on these guys, no chance."

Still, as the Giants started to file out of Comerica Park, it was hard to stifle some of the grins.

"I'm definitely enjoying this," Lincecum said. "It's hard not to." ■

Giants pitcher Ryan Vogelsong gives another masterful performance, throwing 5²/₃ shutout innings to earn the Game 3 win. (Nhat V. Meyer/Staff)

WORLD SERIES: GAME 4
OCTOBER 28, 2012 | GIANTS 4, TIGERS 3, 10 INNINGS

Comeback Complete

S.F. Claims Second Crown In Three Years

By Alex Pavlovic

> **We bought into something you don't see very often. We bought into playing for each other and loving each other.**
>
> — **Right fielder Hunter Pence**

DETROIT—The never-say-die Giants cemented a legacy that will live forever.

After waiting 53 seasons for a first World Series title, San Francisco needed to wait just two for a second. The Giants refused to give in during an often-tumultuous season and refused to let up on the Tigers, sweeping them with a 4-3 win on Sunday.

The 10-inning victory capped one of the most dominant runs in baseball history. After falling behind three games to one in the National League Championship Series, the Giants won seven straight games, outscoring the St. Louis Cardinals and Tigers 36-7.

The final run came on a Marco Scutaro single that scored Ryan Theriot in the top of the 10th inning.

"I'm just glad the whole world got to see what this team is about," Ryan Vogelsong said. "Starting with Game 5 of the NLCS, we played our best baseball of the season. I always knew we were capable of this."

The whole clubhouse felt the same way, and that belief carried a team that overcame injuries and suspensions during the regular season and then won a record six elimination games to reach the World Series. Along the way, the Giants quite simply fell in love with the concept of team.

It was all for one, one for all, symbolized by a hand signal that players would flash at each other on the bases and in the dugout. After big plays, the Giants would put their hands together to form a heart, displaying a kind of love for the

Giants reliever Jeremy Affeldt, who allowed no hits or runs during his 1 2/3 innings in Game 4 of the World Series, throws during the eighth inning. (Gary Reyes/Staff)

game and each other that's rare in Little League, let alone the Big Leagues.

"We bought into something you don't see very often," Hunter Pence said. "We bought into playing for each other and loving each other."

Pence led the emotional charge, delivering raucous pregame speeches that became a staple of the run through the Cincinnati Reds, Cardinals and Tigers. With a 3-0 lead in the World Series, the pregame ceremony — complete with a huddle and sunflower-seed showers — was the same, but the message was different. Several veterans took center stage before the Giants took the Comerica Park field and urged the rest of the team to wrap up the series on this night.

"We knew this was going to be the hardest game," Pence said. "We knew we had to push harder than ever."

They were right. After not trailing for 56 straight innings, the Giants fell behind on Miguel Cabrera's wind-aided two-run blast to right off Matt Cain in the third inning. Buster Posey, the likely National League MVP, later erased the deficit.

Posey had slumped for much of the postseason and didn't have an extra-base hit since a grand slam that spurred a Game 5 victory over the Reds in the NLDS. He had made up for the rough stretch at the plate by guiding a pitching staff that gave up just six World Series runs, the lowest total for a National League pitching staff since 1963.

Giants catcher Buster Posey homers off a changeup from Tigers pitcher Max Scherzer to give San Francisco a 3-2 lead in the sixth inning. (Nhat V. Meyer/Staff)

In the sixth inning, Posey once again stepped into the spotlight at the plate. With a runner at first, he crushed a Max Scherzer changeup through the wind, and like Carlton Fisk in the 1975 World Series, watched closely as the ball curled inside the left field foul pole and gave the Giants a 3-2 lead.

"I was out there leaning for it to stay fair," said Pence, who was on deck. "It was a really cool moment."

The Tigers' Delmon Young soon dashed that moment, hitting a solo shot to right to tie the game in the bottom of the sixth. For several innings, the only big moments belonged to pitchers. Jeremy Affeldt struck out four in a dominant relief stretch, and Phil Coke kept pace for the Tigers.

But in the top of the 10th, the Giants felt that destiny was once again flowing through their dugout. Theriot had lost his job to Scutaro in August and was the surprise choice as D.H. for Game 4. The selection turned out to be one last stroke of genius by manager Bruce Bochy.

Theriot hit a leadoff single off Coke, who had struck out the previous seven Giants he faced in the series. In the dugout, Theriot's teammates looked around in amazement and started punching each other. They all knew Theriot had played for the 2011 champion Cardinals, and more importantly, they all knew Theriot had scored the winning run for LSU in the 2000 college National Championship.

"I knew he would score," Angel Pagan said. "When this guy stopped playing every day, I told him, 'You need to

Giants closer Sergio Romo, who ended the extra innings contest with three consecutive strikeouts, throws a pitch during the ninth inning. (Nhat V. Meyer/Staff)

stay ready. You might be the hero again.'"

First, however, the Giants would need one more hero. After a perfect sacrifice bunt by Brandon Crawford and a strikeout by Pagan, Scutaro stepped to the plate. The MVP of the NLCS is credited for changing the nature of the Giants' lineup after joining the team at the trade deadline, and he showed his famous bat control throughout the postseason. Scutaro swung at 107 pitches in the playoffs and missed just twice. When Coke threw him a fastball on the fifth pitch, Scutaro again found the sweet spot.

His single to center scored Theriot and brought the Giants full circle.

For a group that took pride in being a cohesive unit, this was the ultimate team moment. Theriot had scored the World Series-winning run on a single by the man who took his job, and Theriot couldn't be happier.

"You can't describe the way we came together," Theriot said. "I've never seen anything like it."

The Giants had a unique group in 2010, and closer Brian Wilson capped that memorable run with a strikeout. On Sunday, the new bearded closer, Sergio Romo, ended the season with three straight strikeouts in the bottom of the 10th, getting Triple Crown winner Cabrera looking to end it.

The team that made a habit of pregame huddles and fiery speeches came together one last time, this time on the pitcher's mound. There were no more hurdles to leap, no more comebacks to make.

The Giants were champions, and they didn't need a speech to figure out what would come next.

"Let's prepare for that parade," Pence said, smiling. "It's time to celebrate." ■

Hunter Pence and Brandon Crawford douse Marco Scutaro with champagne. Scutaro, a mid-season acquisition from the Colorado Rockies, had the game-winning RBI during Game 4 of the World Series. (Karl Mondon/Staff)

WORLD SERIES MVP
Kung Fu Panda Takes Home Trophy

By Carl Steward and Mike Lefkow

DETROIT—The Kung Fu Panda stole the show.

Giants third baseman Pablo Sandoval was named World Series MVP on Sunday after the team's sweep of the World Series. The rotund switch hitter gobbled up Detroit Tigers pitching with a .500 batting average, three home runs in Game 1 and four RBIs.

Quite a turnaround for a man who played in only one World Series game two years ago, when the Giants won their first championship since moving to San Francisco by taking four of five games from the Texas Rangers.

"You learn," Sandoval said. "You learn from everything that happened in your career. We're working hard to enjoy this moment right now."

Sandoval had his ups and downs this season as well, including two stints on the disabled list, one with a broken hamate bone, the other a strained hamstring.

But he turned it on throughout the postseason, hitting .364 with six homers and 13 RBIs in 16 games. He also played strong defense at third.

"I (had) surgery again, and I lost muscle, I lost strength," Sandoval said. "But I think the strength came back at the right moment. All the pressure I put on myself to get my strength back, things finally came together."

And in a World Series that numbered nine Venezuelans, including American League Triple Crown winner Miguel Cabrera of the Tigers, Sandoval became the first Venezuelan-born player to be named World Series MVP.

Sandoval preferred to single out his own Venezuelan teammates as opposed to getting the better of perhaps the most feared hitter in the game.

"You know, I'm happy to have two teammates from Venezuela, one the clutch hitter (Marco Scutaro) and the other one the Gold Glove (Gregor Blanco)," he said. "I was just happy to be part of the group, the beautiful group we got here."

Sandoval gives much of the credit for his development to manager Bruce Bochy and general manager Brian Sabean.

"When you have a good manager, good G.M., throwing all the things in your face, you have to keep focused and keep playing and keep working hard," Sandoval said.

His best moment in the postseason came in Game 1 of the World Series, when he belted homers in his first three at-bats to lead an 8-3 Giants victory.

"You know, I still can't believe that game," he said. "It's the game of your dreams. You don't want to wake up."

Only three other players have hit three homers in a World Series game. Hall of Famer Babe Ruth did it twice. Reggie Jackson, who is also in the Hall of Fame, and Albert Pujols each did it once.

Now the world knows the Panda, and he could only thank Barry Zito, who originally gave him the moniker.

"When I got that nickname, I think, it's me," he said. "The character is me — have fun like a little kid, fight for

Giants third baseman Pablo Sandoval celebrates with the MVP Trophy. Sandoval, the first Venezuelan-born player to win the award, hit .500 with three home runs during the World Series. (Nhat V. Meyer/Staff)

The Giants take a victory lap after their 8-4 win over the San Diego Padres on September 22. That victory clinched the Giants' second National League West crown in three years. (Jim Gensheimer/Staff)

Offseason Moves Designed to Give Pitching a Hand

Giants Expect an Improved Offense in 2012

By Alex Pavlovic

Newly acquired center fielder Angel Pagan said the Giants' pitchers had a well-established reputation throughout the National League last season, one the position players could benefit from.

"We all knew that every time you put three or four runs on the board, this pitching staff will fight like an upside-down cat to protect it," Pagan said. "As a hitter, you have to fight the same way."

The Giants were last in the N.L. in runs scored last season with a mere 570. In the all-important quest to provide their dominant pitching staff with more support, they are counting on three things to happen:

Pagan and fellow newcomers Melky Cabrera and Gregor Blanco will need to set the table for the middle of the order.

The Giants are hoping their health returns. The team used the disabled list a major league-high 25 times last season, the most notable absence being catcher Buster Posey, who missed 114 games with a broken leg and torn ankle ligaments after a home-plate collision with Scott Cousins.

But Posey is back and once again is in the heart of the lineup.

"With all the guys that got hurt, we were basically a whole new lineup last season," first baseman Aubrey Huff said. "To be back and healthy is a big plus, and that's all you can ask for. As long as you're healthy, good things can happen."

Huff is smack dab in the middle of the third key: Like several others, he needs to have a better season. Huff rewarded a two-year, $22 million contract and 579 plate appearances last year with a .246 average and 12 home runs.

But after returning to his pre-2010 workout routine, Huff said he's ready for a bounce-back year.

"I'm coming out with a positive mind frame, and I'm ready to go," he said.

The Giants also are counting on more production from youngsters Brandon Belt and Brandon Crawford.

Belt hit just .225 as a rookie, though he did show some promise with nine home runs in 187 at-bats. It might not happen right away, but Belt is expected to eventually help anchor the middle of the lineup.

Crawford has been handed the starting job at short despite hitting .204 as a rookie, but the Giants tweaked his swing and were pleased with his .340 average and three home runs in Cactus League play.

General manager Brian Sabean speaks at a rally following the Giants' triumph in the 2010 World Series. Sabean, the team's general manager since 1996, acquired key contributors Angel Pagan and Melky Cabrera before the 2012 season and added veterans Hunter Pence and Marco Scutaro in mid-season. (Patrick Tehan/Staff)

> "This is what West Coast baseball is all about — let's run and use our speed and manufacture runs. The excitement we've seen on the bases gets pitchers thinking. Having a fast team like we do can put pressure on pitchers, and I think that's kind of how we want to play." — **Pitcher Tim Lincecum**

Add it all up, and the team believes it will be much improved at the plate. Given last year's meager results, it wouldn't take much to find improvement.

The Giants hit a major league low .219 with runners in scoring position last season and averaged the fourth-fewest runs per game in club history. For a team that had over half of its games decided by one or two runs, the lack of offense brought the World Series champions' repeat bid to a slow and painful end.

Within the clubhouse, many believe those results were a fluke, even members of the run-starved pitching staff.

"I think that even if we kept the same team, we would have been better offensively than last year, " left-hander Madison Bumgarner said. "It was bad luck more than anything."

The front office felt differently.

General manager Brian Sabean moved quickly in the offseason. He traded talented-but-erratic left-hander Jonathan Sanchez to the Kansas City Royals for Cabrera, then sent center fielder Andres Torres and right-handed reliever Ramon Ramirez to the New York Mets for Pagan.

At the urging of hitting coach Hensley Meulens, the Giants also signed Blanco out of the Venezuelan winter league.

The former Atlanta Brave and Royal ended up winning a job with a strong spring and could push Pagan for the leadoff role. He didn't play in the majors last year, but he hit .283 in a part-time role with the Braves and Royals in 2010, and he had 74 walks and 13 steals in a full-time role with Atlanta in 2008.

Pagan is a .279 career hitter and stole 69 bases the last two seasons but showed neither of those skills this spring. Nonetheless, the Giants will give him every opportunity to provide the spark that Torres brought in 2010.

"We're looking at him to be a catalyst," manager Bruce Bochy said. "It's very exciting, the burst of speed he has. He makes us more athletic."

Cabrera does the same, and looks poised to build on a breakthrough 2011 season, when he set career highs with 18 homers, 44 doubles, 87 RBIs and 20 stolen bases.

Cabrera stayed hot this spring, and his speed and extra-base power could fit anywhere from the leadoff spot to the heart of the order.

"That's what West Coast baseball is all about — let's run and use our speed and manufacture runs, " opening day starter Tim Lincecum said. "The excitement we've seen on the bases gets pitchers thinking. Having a fast team like we do can put pressure on pitchers, and I think that's kind of how we want to play."

A few extra runs — manufactured or otherwise — could do wonders for Lincecum, who had a 2.74 ERA but finished with a 13-14 record last season, largely because he received one run or fewer in 16 of his 33 starts.

Pagan wasn't around for any of that, but he knows the math isn't difficult: The Giants were 55-9 when they scored at least four runs last season.

"This team committed to getting back to the playoffs by putting some speed at the top of the lineup and adding some power," Pagan said. "If we can provide some runs early in games, with this pitching staff, it's over." ∎

Angel Pagan slides home to score on a sacrifice fly during a May game against the Cardinals. Pagan's speed was central to the Giants' attack — he finished the 2012 season with 29 stolen bases and a league-leading 15 triples. (Josie Lepe/Staff)

#28
CATCHER

BUSTER POSEY

Giants Missed Their Star Catcher Almost as Much as He Missed the Game

Daniel Brown • April 6, 2012

As a kid, Buster Posey wrote a poem about watching a baseball sail over a fence. As a college player, he prepared for the rigors of his position by settling into a catcher's crouch to watch games on TV. When he got married in 2010, the recessional music was "Take Me Out to the Ballgame."

Think baseball suffered without Posey last year? Not as much as Posey suffered without baseball.

"You miss being on the field. You miss the guys. You miss the crowd. You just miss the game in general," he said. "You miss everything about it."

At long last Posey is back, bringing with him the Giants' hopes of another season that ends in champagne. He will be behind the plate Friday for the season opener against the Arizona Diamondbacks, capping his return from a home-plate collision in May that left Posey with torn ligaments, a fractured fibula and a broken heart.

That injury not only knocked Posey out for the remainder of the season but also seemed to break the Giants' magic spell. Their mysticism of beards and misfits and golden thongs gave way to a humdrum squad that finished eight games out in the National League West.

With Posey: 27-21 and in first place.

Without him: 59-55 with an offense so quiet that it could take batting practice in a library and not merit a "shush."

Fans, recognizing Posey's value to the franchise, welcomed him back with a rollicking ovation Monday night simply for trotting out to his position. Never mind that this was an exhibition game. It sounded like October.

"That was quite a special moment. You could feel all the energy in the crowd," closer Brian Wilson said. "And it was well-deserved. Buster has battled. He's come back healthy."

"And he's checked off every box he can to alleviate any doubt. He's ready to rock. He's ready to go."

First baseman Brandon Belt said: "Pretty much everybody in the city loves him. His teammates feel the same way."

With so much hinging on Posey's return, it's easy to forget that he has just 585 career at-bats. He's never played more than 108 games in a big-league regular season.

But teammates say it's not just his production. It's his presence. From the day he arrived in the big leagues,

Buster Posey singles in the eighth inning of Game 1 of the National League Division Series. Posey led the National League with a .336 batting average. (Nhat V. Meyer/Staff)

"I think being away hurt him pretty bad. As a player, you're so used to being with those guys, playing every day and feeling that competitive drive." — **Kristen Posey**

Posey has been a grizzled catcher in a young man's body. (He was the first rookie backstop ever to bat cleanup in a postseason game.)

"He gets overlooked for his work behind the plate because he swings the bat so well," pitcher Matt Cain said. "But he caught on to the game-calling so quickly that he just took over the staff. He wasn't worried about calling any kind of pitch in any count."

Reliever Jeremy Affeldt, a 10-year vet, said, "He's probably one of the smarter game-callers I've seen, especially for someone who has such limited time in the big leagues."

He has same effect in the lineup, where his importance seems disproportionate for a player with 22 career home runs. But with Posey batting No. 4 last season, the Giants went 21-15, by far their best mark among their regular cleanup hitters. They went 25-26 with Aubrey Huff batting fourth and 15-21 with Pablo Sandoval there.

With Posey back, the lineup returns to its natural order.

"Now you have three-hole hitters and five-hole hitters who aren't up there trying to hit four-run homers," Affeldt said. "They're just trying to get on base, maybe drive in some runs, protect a little bit."

One reliable scouting source (his wife) reports that Posey arrived to spring training even more mature, a development that stems not from taking on the Dodgers and Diamondbacks but from an extended homestand with the twins.

Buster and Kristen welcomed Lee Dempsey (a son) and Addison Lynn (daughter) Aug. 14. Buster was able to set aside the mask and focus on fatherhood. It was the first time Kristen had seen her high school sweetheart without baseball.

"It's a whirlwind, a huge change, to say the least, when you have two babies who are totally dependent on you," she said.

Still, seeing Buster without baseball for the first time was unsettling. She joked that she could look at him at times and tell he was thinking about how to improve his swing.

"I think being away hurt him pretty bad," she said. "As a player, you're so used to being with those guys, playing every day and feeling that competitive drive."

Now that he's back, Posey looks rejuvenated. He went so far as to call himself "lucky" because of the way the Giants managed his physical rehabilitation. His last major medical procedure was July 22, when he had surgery to remove screws from his left ankle.

"It seems like it went by pretty fast," Posey said. "They never let me get too far ahead (in my thinking) and kind of stayed on the task at hand."

Before the injury, Posey was durable. He started 43 of the Giants' first 48 games — 41 at catcher and two at first base. Manager Bruce Bochy said Wednesday that he plans to give Posey frequent breaks from behind home plate, including entire games on the bench.

But having been out of baseball for nearly a year, Posey is eager to make up for lost time. When he takes the field for opening night Friday, his long road to recovery will be complete.

"I think it's over. It's done," Posey said. "It's time to get going." ■

Catcher Buster Posey celebrates with reliever Sergio Romo after Romo closed out the Giants' win over the Cardinals in Game 6 of the National League Championship Series. Posey is respected as much for his handling of the Giants pitching staff as he is for his offense. (Gary Reyes/Staff)

Wilson Shelved for the Year

Closer Has Structural Damage in Pitching Elbow

By Carl Steward

Eight games into the 2012 season, the Giants have suffered a potentially devastating injury. Closer Brian Wilson is facing likely elbow surgery and might be lost for the season.

An MRI on Friday night revealed that Wilson has "structural issues" with the ligament in his right elbow, manager Bruce Bochy said Saturday before the Giants' 4-3 victory over the Pittsburgh Pirates at AT&T Park. Wilson has been placed on the 15-day disabled list, but he's probably going to be out a lot longer.

After a 32-pitch inning against Colorado on Thursday in which he struggled to get the save during a 4-2 Giants' win, Wilson complained of elbow stiffness Friday. Subsequent tests revealed structural damage.

Bochy and trainer Dave Groeschner said Wilson would be examined by team orthopedist Dr. Ken Akizuki and that calls then would be made to set up second and third opinions, including from noted Pensacola, Fla., elbow surgeon Dr. James Andrews, before making a final determination about surgery.

The manager did not sound optimistic.

"After the tests (Friday), it doesn't look very good right now," Bochy said. "He'll get a couple more opinions, but he's likely facing surgery, to be honest."

There have been questions about Wilson's health since he blew a save in a 5-4 walk-off loss to Atlanta on Aug. 15. Wilson was examined by Andrews two days later and placed on the disabled list Aug. 21 with inflammation in the elbow. He was reinstated Sept. 18 but appeared in just two games before being shut down for the remainder of the season.

During spring training, Wilson said the late-season shutdown was done for precautionary reasons and that there were no issues with the elbow.

"I am healthy, and I'm doing everything I can to make sure everyone is aware of that," he said March 26. "(The elbow) wasn't a concern for me."

Wilson, who turned 30 last month, made six appearances in spring training, throwing $5\frac{1}{3}$ innings with no earned runs allowed, two walks and eight strikeouts.

He made his regular-season debut Wednesday, pitching the eighth inning of a 17-8 loss in Denver. He gave up a run on one hit and one walk, throwing 24 pitches.

Wilson's second outing of the season was even more difficult. He loaded the bases and walked in a run before preserving a 4-2 victory. At one point, Bochy and Groeschner, along with catcher Buster Posey, came out to check on Wilson. He took a warm-up pitch and finished the game, and afterward, Bochy said Wilson had tweaked his left ankle. His velocity declined noticeably during the inning.

Groeschner said the elbow issue became apparent Friday afternoon when Wilson went through his pregame routine.

"Even though he was off, he still had to throw and prepare," the trainer said. "That's when he came and talked to us."

Said Bochy: "I feel for Willie. He's worked hard with rehab, and he'd come a long way. We checked off every box with him, back-to-back days, everything. I think he was all set to go, and then this happens, so it's a disappointing day for Willie personally, and then obviously the team."

Wilson was not available for comment, but Bochy spoke with him.

"I'm sure he's disappointed with what's happened, and we all feel terrible," the manager said. "But he said, 'Hey, I'll be back to help you guys.'"

Wilson has 171 career saves, including 36 last season.

He led the majors with 48 saves in 2010 and had six more in the postseason, including closing out all three series-clinching wins en route to the Giants' first World Series victory in San Francisco.

Bochy said Ryan Vogelsong, who was scheduled to come off the disabled list Sunday to make his first start of the season, would replace Wilson on the roster.

As for how Wilson would be replaced in the bullpen, Bochy said it would be a closer by committee for the time being.

"It'll be similar to last year when Willie was out," he said. "We'll use everybody, go with the hot hand. (Santiago) Casilla may be saving some games. (Sergio) Romo and (Javier) Lopez, we think we're in good hands there. That's the game plan right now." ■

Brian Wilson watches the final inning of the Giants' win over the Cardinals in Game 5 of the National League Championship Series. The Giants' closer and one of the team's most colorful personalities pitched in just two games in 2012 before an elbow injury ended his season in April. (Karl Mondon/Staff)

#54
PITCHER

SERGIO ROMO

Border Town of Brawley Celebrates Romo's Success

By Elliott Almond • October 27, 2012

The outside world seems so far away from the dusty town Sergio Romo calls home. Located at the floor of California, Brawley is an economically depressed community of 25,000 residents surrounded by fields of sugar beets, melons and lettuce.

But this week the Great Beyond feels a lot closer as the lovable Giants reliever employs his wicked slider against the Detroit Tigers in the World Series. Romo's emergence as San Francisco's savior is amplified in this desolate region where the mien tilts decidedly south to the Baja scrublands a short drive from here.

"He put Brawley on the map," said Rusty Garcia, a member of the city's district board of education. "Even people who don't know him have adopted him. Everybody has this little glow."

Brawley needed a folk hero about now. A swarm of earthquakes in late August damaged buildings in Imperial Valley, including Brawley Union High's auditorium that is now closed for a year. Then two separate fires in recent weeks destroyed a 60-year-old family run furniture store and a bar in downtown.

No wonder the bartender at Las Chabelas Mexican restaurant rang a bell Thursday night as soon as Romo got the final out to preserve the Giants' 2-0 victory in Game 2. Among the patrons leading cheers were Mayor George A. Nava and state assemblyman V. Manuel Perez (D-Coachella).

A few hours earlier, Romo's high school coach, Pedro Carranza, stood in a blazing autumn sun at Eddie Wiest Field watching his three-time defending league champions run through drills.

"It's not the game but what it represents," Carranza said. "I don't think Sergio understands the magnitude of what he's doing."

Baseball has been part of the fiber that has connected this tortilla flat valley for generations. That has never wavered, though Brawley is a football town with the requisite imagery of "Friday Night Lights."

Carranza played in the minors with the Colorado Rockies and later in the Mexican League. He is one of almost two dozen Brawley-bred athletes who have played professionally.

The list includes Sid Monge, Rudy Seanez, Steve Whitehead and Andrew Romo, Sergio's brother.

Giants pitcher Sergio Romo lets out a scream after finishing off the St. Louis Cardinals to take Game 7 of the National League Championship Series. (Susan Tripp Pollar/Staff)

Whitehead teaches at Brawley High. Seanez opened a training facility in nearby Imperial where he hopes to develop the next generation of ballplayers. Monge coaches in Mexico.

One of Brawley High's bigger players is Eddie Espinoza, 17, who is Romo's second cousin. Senior catcher C.J. Perez also knows the Giants reliever. His dad is close friends with Sergio's father, Frank Romo.

"My dad said Sergio always had heart," said C.J., who like Romo has dreamed of being a big leaguer since childhood.

Romo's exploits are energizing the current crop of Brawley kids.

"It makes you think you could do this, too," said Perez, who has a 3.7 grade-point average. "It's my turn."

Perez already walks along a path Romo once tread. It goes in the opposite direction of the well-played immigration trail to El Norte.

Brawley's baseball success has been attributed to the opportunities afforded players in Mexicali, Mexico, 22 miles due south on CA 111.

Mexican Americans from the Imperial Valley have been crossing the border to play winter ball for generations. Frank Romo did it as a child. He later brought Sergio and Andrew with him.

And he's still doing it at 55 in Mexico's Veterans League. He's just not going to play this weekend because of the World Series.

"There were times I'd play Monday and Wednesday in Brawley, Tuesday and Thursday in El Centro and the weekends in Mexicali," Frank Romo said.

Seanez, who played for nine teams in a lengthy career as a big league reliever, said the severe conditions of Mexican ballparks helped shaped American kids. They played on dirt with sacks used as base bags.

"They played as if the game meant something," said Seanez, who often joined the Romos in Winter League games in Mexico.

Giants reliever Sergio Romo, known for his long, dark beard, throws a pitch during the ninth inning of Game 6 of the National League Championship Series. (Nhat V. Meyer/Staff)

> "He put Brawley on the map. Even people who don't know him have adopted him. Everybody has this little glow."

— Rusty Garcia

Carranza, the Brawley high coach, did as well. "If you can catch a ground ball down there, you can field a ball almost anywhere," he said.

Mexicali is where Sergio Romo learned to be fearless. Playing against men forced the teens to mature quickly.

"It teaches you you're not always going to be the best — even when you've still got your good stuff," Seanez said. "It stays with you."

It stuck with Romo.

An *Imperial Valley Press* editorial this week said "a skinny guy with intense eyes, a huge black beard and an animated demeanor more likely would find fame as a member of a heavy metal band than as an athlete."

But for all the theatrics, Romo personifies his community as a humble, hardworking guy. He is one of baseball's most genuine players while serving as the Giants' No. 1 ambassador. Every first-pitch ceremony at AT&T Park ends with him catching the ball and presenting it to the honored guest. Every fun TV spot the Giants have done the past two seasons has centered on the gregarious reliever.

"That's the type of people you are going to meet out here," said Nava, Brawley's mayor and a San Jose State graduate.

All of this started with Frank Romo, who seemingly played with everybody who's anybody in the Valley. His father was good enough to play for the Diablos, Mexico's New York Yankees. But he had to work on the family ranch in Jalisco, and later worked the fields in California.

Frank's baseball career also was cut short being the son of an immigrant farmworker. The family used to pick produce from the Imperial Valley to Salinas.

The time in Salinas led Frank to follow the Giants. But his father stuck with the Dodgers, the team Imperial Valley supports although the San Diego Padres play two hours to the west and the Arizona Diamondbacks are four hours to the northeast.

Frank Romo wanted a different route for his boys

as he created a steady life in Brawley as a machinist for the Imperial Irrigation District. He built a Little League pitching mound in the back yard of their house on a quiet corner on Brawley's east side.

The father taught his son some of the mechanics of throwing, though he never pitched like Sergio's grandfather.

"It was in him," Frank Romo recalled of Sergio, who at 5-foot-10 and 183 pounds often was told he was too small to have a baseball a career.

Then Frank added, "I'd be lying if I say I'd imagine it."

Romo, 29, traveled a long road since graduating from Brawley High in 2001. He spent a year each at Orange Coast College, Arizona Western, North Alabama and Mesa State in Colorado. At almost every turn, someone from Brawley such as Carranza had a hand in helping him move forward.

But Romo just wasn't going to quit.

"Sergio wanted it bad, and nobody was going to stop him," his father said.

The Giants drafted Romo in 2005. The reliever made his major league debut in 2008 and became a hit two years later as San Francisco's primary setup pitcher. During the 2010 World Series, Romo became popular as one of the Giants' "Beards" led by closer Brian Wilson.

Romo's legend has grown in these parts since he replaced Santiago Casilla, the first man to step into the closer's role after Wilson's season-ending injury in April.

But at home Leticia Romo is waiting for her son to fulfill a promise — to fix a window he allegedly broke while throwing in the back yard as a kid.

The Romos told their son once he made it in the majors he could return to fix it. But Sergio claims he isn't guilty while also refusing to say who is.

Frank Romo isn't buying it to this day.

"We know he broke it," the father said.

But his voice gives Frank Romo away. All is forgiven.

Perfect!

Matt Cain Fans 14, Pitches First Perfect Game in Giants History

By Alex Pavlovic

SAN FRANCISCO—Matt Cain has talked openly of his lifelong dream of throwing a perfect game. It's no longer just a dream.

Cain threw the first perfect game in the Giants' long and storied history Wednesday night at AT&T Park, striking out 14 and getting great defensive plays from outfielders Melky Cabrera and Gregor Blanco in a 10-0 victory over the Houston Astros.

Cain, the longest-tenured Giant, has been through it all in his eight seasons in San Francisco. He has seen highs — a World Series title in 2010 — and lows — dozens of losses on nights when he was brilliant.

Through it all, Cain has been unflappable, but that trait never has been tested as it was Wednesday night.

"There's really nothing like it," said Cain, who previously had taken five no-hitters into the seventh inning and had a perfect game into the sixth inning of his second start this season.

"I was having to recheck myself to see the signs that Buster (Posey) was putting down. I was thinking about it. It felt like it was the World Series, but it almost felt a little louder."

Cain was the one providing the impetus for most of the noise. His day started in unorthodox fashion, when he took an impromptu swing during a pregame golf ex-

hibition and drove a ball 300 yards into McCovey Cove.

In retrospect, that perfect swing should have been a sign of things to come.

Cain mowed down the Astros from the outset, establishing all of his pitches, especially a fastball that stymied the Astros throughout.

"The first time through the lineup, I felt like something could happen," he said.

With plenty of help from his own lineup and a couple stunning plays from his defense, Cain sailed into the ninth inning.

Brian Bogusevic and Chris Snyder flied out for the first two outs of the ninth, and as the sellout crowd held its collective breath, Cain got Jason Castro to ground out to third.

Twenty-seven up. Twenty-seven down.

Cain, beloved by teammates and a fan base that rejoiced when he signed a new six-year contract in April, was mobbed on the mound.

"I just hugged him and he said, 'This is stupid,'" manager Bruce Bochy said. "I think he understood how much we think of him and the game he threw."

Cain's perfect game was just the 22nd in major league history (counting the postseason) and the second of the 2012 season. Chicago White Sox right-hander Philip Humber threw a perfect game on April 21. Cain's effort was the

Giants pitcher Matt Cain embraces his catcher, Buster Posey, after accomplishing perfection against the Houston Astros. (AP Images)

first no-hit performance by a Giant since Jonathan Sanchez no-hit the San Diego Padres on July 10, 2009.

Cain, 27, took the dominance a step further, tying Sandy Koufax's record for strikeouts in a perfect game.

He did what Hall of Famers and Cy Young Award winners never could while donning the orange and black.

"It's such a hard thing to do — to be a part of it is special, a night we will all remember," Bochy said. "He's had some hard luck in the past, and he's been close. For him to be the guy that gets it makes it all the more special."

The first five innings featured little drama for Cain, who repeatedly threw first-pitch strikes to an Astros lineup that was caught looking time after time. But like any bid for history, there would be moments when the defense was tested.

Cabrera made the first highlight play of the night, a leaping grab that secured the second out of the sixth inning. Snyder's blast to left looked like it would easily travel into the left-field bleachers, but the thick San Francisco air knocked the ball down and gave Cabrera time to make the catch just inches in front of the wall.

"I thought it was gone," Bochy said. "It seemed like it almost went over the wall and came back."

"Oh yeah," Cain said, nodding his head emphatically. "I thought it was a homer. I have no idea why that ball stayed in the park."

History was tested again in the seventh when Jordan Schafer led off with a liner deep toward Triples Alley, where home runs go to die but hits rarely do.

Blanco is a center fielder by trade but plays right field in the Giants' loaded alignment. The first-year Giant is fond of saying the outfield features three players with center fielder's skills, and he showed them while chasing Schafer's ball down and making a diving catch on the warning track.

Blanco called it the greatest catch of his life.

"I was aware of what was going on," he said. "I said to myself, 'If it's hit there, you'd better catch it.'"

In the dugout, Bochy couldn't bear to watch.

"I just put my head down and then looked up and saw Blanco and he was relentless," Bochy said. "I think Matt knew something special was happening."

As Blanco held the ball high above his head, a sellout crowd of 42,298 gave him an extended standing ovation. The disbelief was momentary — Cain struck out Jose Altuve and Jed Lowrie to end the seventh.

Bochy pulled out all the stops in the late innings, inserting strong fielders Brandon Crawford and Emmanuel Burriss in the middle infield and moving Joaquin Arias over to third in place of Pablo Sandoval. As Cain's pitch count began to rise, Bochy sent long man Shane Loux behind the dugout to secretly warm up.

"Matt didn't know it," Bochy said. "I had somebody ready. But once it got to the eighth we had no problems. I was going to let Matt go 130 pitches, maybe more."

Cain needed 103 pitches to get through the seventh. Arias, an early-season call-up, easily gloved a slow grounder and made a strong throw to first to retire J.D. Martinez, the first batter of the eighth. Cain went to a 3-2 count on Brett Wallace, one of just four on the night, before striking him out looking with a 93 mph inside fastball.

The 14th strikeout marked a career high for Cain, but bigger things were to come.

Chris Johnson's ground out to short ended the eighth inning, as Cain walked off and quietly took a seat in the dugout with 114 pitches down. Around him, AT&T Park shook as it never has.

"I was as nervous as I've ever been on a baseball field," Posey said.

Posey and the rest of the lineup had taken care of the notoriously hard-luck Cain's run support early, scoring 10 runs through the first five innings. Cabrera, Brandon Belt and Blanco homered, giving the Giants five homers in the last two games. They entered the series with just six homers this season at AT&T Park, but anything seemed possible for the Giants on this night.

Cain proved that on every one of his 125 pitches.

"This is awesome," he said. "I can't explain what the guys did to make this happen. Everybody did a lot of work.

"It turned out perfect." ■

San Francisco mayor Ed Lee presents Matt Cain with a key to the city during a June 26 ceremony at AT&T Park honoring Cain's perfect game.

#18
PITCHER

MATT CAIN

Secret's Out: Cain Is Among the Best

Monte Poole • June 15, 2012

His tale was that of a man who would pitch like a champ, get little or no help from his lineup and shrug off the absence of backup. His teammates would sigh, the locals would despair and a nation of baseball fans would barely notice.

This has been the primary theme of Matt Cain's Giants career, persisting through 215 starts, two All-Star game selections and a championship postseason in which he did not allow an earned run in three starts.

The long overdue update on Cain's marquee worthiness is now being demanded.

With a perfect game against Houston on Wednesday night, in his 216th start, Cain submitted the best possible attempt to rewrite the narrative.

"It's been something I've always wanted to do, ever since I was little," Cain said Thursday, 14 hours after his champagne-soaked moment. "I've always wanted to have that on my résumé. To finally have it is ... pretty amazing."

The big right-hander was both impeccable and historic in pitching the first perfect game in 128 years of Giants baseball and the 22nd since the game was conceived in the middle of the 19th century.

This ought to be enough to free Cain from the imposing accomplishments of two-time Cy Young Award winner Tim Lincecum. This should to be enough to liberate Cain from the lies being spread by his mediocre career win-loss record. This has to be enough to convince a nation of fans that when roll is called for the game's best active pitchers, his name deserves to be announced very early in the process.

"I've said all along that this guy's a No. 1," manager Bruce Bochy said.

I've had clubhouse conversations in recent years with numerous opposing batters raving about Lincecum, then raving more loudly about Cain. At least two have said they don't look forward to either one, but they'd rather avoid Cain if they had a choice.

And many of those comments were made before this season, when Cain finally pushed his career record above .500 while Lincecum has struggled.

With Cain, however, the numbers have had a tendency to spread lies. And those lies were abetted by the Giants' tendency to score little or not at all with Cain on the mound.

Matt Cain delivers a pitch during the first inning of the Giants' Game 5 win over the Reds in the National League Division Series. Cain won a career-high 16 games in 2012. (Patrick Tehan/Staff)

In the years since Cain made his major league debut in 2005, no starter in baseball has received less run support. In the four years leading up to San Francisco's world championship season in 2010, Cain was one of 17 pitchers whose career ERA was under 3.50 — and the only one without a winning record.

"It's a wonder he hasn't lost all the marbles in his head, all those times he got nothing because we didn't score for him," general manager Brian Sabean said. "It's a testament to the kind of person he is that he never once complained or even mentioned it. He's as grounded as anyone we have, in just about every way."

The ESPN.com website, promoting a story Thursday about the improved pitching in baseball, featured drawings of five pitchers: Detroit's Justin Verlander, Seattle's Felix Hernandez, Texas' Yu Darvish, Washington's Stephen Strasburg and the Dodgers' Clayton Kershaw.

This is the kind of negligence that needs to change and is bound to get corrected as the perfect game sinks in.

The measure of Cain, the pitcher, has long been evident, revealed in how wonderfully tolerant he has been on those many days when his teammates failed him. We're used to seeing him excel without reward.

He needed only minimum assistance Wednesday. The perfect game is a pitcher's statement, that he will not be beaten. Cain earned it, not only with one game on one night but with unwavering dedication under conceivably demoralizing conditions.

"Couldn't happen to a better guy," Sabean said. "I've always considered him our John Wayne, kind of a big, reliable hero. Lincecum is our Johnny Depp, but Cain is our rock."

Cain has spent his career as baseball's best unheralded pitcher. The Giants recognized that when they signed him in April to a five-year extension worth $112.5 million.

Now it's time for everyone else to notice. How could anyone not? ∎

Opposite: Giants pitcher Matt Cain, who led the team in wins, ERA and strikeouts during the regular season, throws during the first inning of Game 1 of the NLDS. (Jim Gensheimer/Staff) Above: Matt Cain delivers a pitch against the Cardinals in Game 7 of the National League Championship Series. The Giants stretched both rounds of the National League playoffs to deciding games, and their ace collected the win in both winner-take-all matchups. (Nhat V. Meyer/Staff)

Giant Romp
S.F. Stars Deliver Rebuttal to N.Y. Critics

By Daniel Brown

KANSAS CITY, Mo.—To repay the fans who stuffed the ballot box, the Giants stuffed the box score Tuesday night.

Melky Cabrera, Pablo Sandoval, Buster Posey and Matt Cain propelled the National League to an 8-0 victory in the 83rd All-Star game at Kauffman Stadium, silencing a weeklong uproar from a sour Big Apple.

Sandoval, who surpassed Mets third baseman David Wright in the controversial final balloting, hit a three-run triple to key a five-run first inning.

Cain, who got the starting nod over Mets pitcher R.A. Dickey, pitched two scoreless innings and became the first Giants pitcher to win an All-Star game since Vida Blue in 1981.

And Cabrera, the former Royal making a triumphant return to Kansas City, had a rally-starting single and a two-run homer. The N.L. center fielder became the first Giants player to win MVP honors since Bobby Bonds in 1973, also in Kansas City.

"I didn't come to win an MVP," Cabrera said. "That's just a surprise. It's a great gift that the Lord gave me.

"But the opportunity that Kansas City gave me last year is the same opportunity that San Francisco is giving me every day to showcase my talent."

This marked just seventh time in All-Star history that both the MVP and the winning pitcher came from the same team. It also gave the Giants a retort to those who accused the fan base of voting in undeserving players.

"We were trying to show the fans that we support them," Sandoval said.

"I can't thank fans enough for voting these guys in," Cain said.

The N.L. now has its first three-game winning streak since 1994-96 and, as per the new tradition, secured home-field advantage for the World Series.

In all, Giants hitters combined to go 3 for 7 with a home run, a triple, five RBI and four runs, an onslaught that made it a tossup as to whether Sandoval or Cabrera would win the MVP award.

To celebrate his honor, Cabrera brought his mother and grandmother to the news conference podium. He spoke as mom dabbed away tears.

"It's a gift to have them here," Cabrera said.

Cabrera started the first-inning scoring parade by blazing out of the batter's box in his Nike neon-orange cleats.

Seeing no need to savor his first career All-Star at-bat, Cabrera smacked the first pitch he saw, a 98 mph

Giants outfielder Melky Cabrera, who played for the Kansas City Royals in 2011, shows off his MVP trophy after the All-Star Game in Kansas City, Missouri. (AP Images)

fastball from Justin Verlander, to left field for a one-out single. He scored on Ryan Braun's double to make it 1-0.

Verlander struggled with his control after that, walking Carlos Beltran and Posey to load the bases. Sandoval noticed that the Tigers ace was struggling with his fastball, so he was ready when Verlander tried a curve.

Sandoval lashed the ball into the right-field corner for a three-run triple. By the time Sandoval chugged into third, the N.L. led 4-0.

"The back-breaker," N.L. manager Tony La Russa called it.

In an unlikely development, Sandoval joined Mel Ott (1938) and Willie Mays ('57, '59, '60) as Giants players to hit a triple in an All-Star game.

"I didn't know where the ball was going to end up," Sandoval said, "so I just put my head down and ran."

The five-run first tied an N.L. record for most runs in an inning. After that, the only drama was the final margin of victory. Cabrera, who scored the game's first run, also scored the last: He homered with Matt Holliday aboard in the fourth.

In doing so, Cabrera joined seven other Giants players with All-Star home runs: Johnny Mize (1947), Mays ('56, '60 and '65), Willie McCovey (two in '69), Dick Dietz ('70), Bobby Bonds ('73), Will Clark ('92) and Barry Bonds ('98, '02).

Cain and the rest of the N.L. pitchers delivered zeros. This was the first All-Star shutout since the N.L. won 6-0 in 1996 in Philadelphia. The eight-run margin of victory was the largest by either team since the A.L. won 13-3 at Comiskey Park in Chicago in 1983.

Cain breezed through his two innings in part because his nerves were eased by the 5-0 lead built by a few familiar faces.

"It's always fun to watch Pablo run the bases," he said. ∎

Giants players (clockwise) Pablo Sandoval, Matt Cain and Melky Cabrera helped the National League win the All-Star Game, earning the Giants home-field advantage in the World Series. (AP Images)

#19
SECOND BASE

MARCO SCUTARO

Veteran Scutaro Has Been a Magician at the Plate for the Giants

Alex Pavlovic • September 14, 2012

I n the Giants dugout, Marco Scutaro's teammates had a hard time believing what they just had just seen. Colorado right-hander Alex White threw two fastballs past Scutaro and struck him out.

Since being traded to the Giants on July 27, Scutaro has swung and missed just nine times in 198 plate appearances. It's a stat that has teammates marveling.

"It's amazing," said leadoff hitter Angel Pagan, who has caught fire with Scutaro hitting behind him. "It's something we've all been talking about."

"I heard that number and I couldn't believe it," said shortstop Brandon Crawford, Scutaro's partner in the middle of the infield. "You're going to have off days in this game, and he hasn't."

Hitting coach Hensley Meulens called Scutaro one of the most technically sound hitters he has ever worked with.

"He's got a short swing and he doesn't try to do too much with a pitch," Meulens said. "He's just short to it and long through it. That's what you try and teach. If I could clone him, I would do it. Those are perfect mechanics."

In a race that's featured one flashy acquisition after another — mostly by the rival Los Angeles Dodgers — the 36-year-old Scutaro has been the biggest prize. The Giants are 26-18 since his arrival and have pulled away in the National League West, in large part because of Scutaro's .341 average and 30 RBIs since arriving.

The quick bat and calm approach have made Scutaro a nightmare for opposing pitchers. But for Scutaro, this is a way of playing that has been honed during a long, winding career that has taken him through eight organizations since he signed out of Venezuela in 1994.

"I just try to stay on my game — and I know my game," Scutaro said. "I'm not a power hitter. I'm not an RBI guy. I just try and have good at-bats and get on base."

Since breaking through with the A's in 2004, Scutaro has done just that. He had a .350 on-base percentage in 2006 and seemingly was a poster child for what the Moneyball A's were trying to build. But the A's traded him to the Toronto Blue Jays a year later.

Scutaro signed with Boston before the 2010 season but was traded to the Rockies last offseason despite two productive seasons with the Red Sox. The Rockies fell

Giants infielder Marco Scutaro, acquired from the Colorado Rockies during mid-season, forces Matt Holliday out at second base during Game 2 of the National League Championship Series. Scutaro was injured on the play and left the game, but returned to contribute clutch hitting later in the series. (Jose Carlos Fajardo/Staff)

> **"I just try to stay on my game — and I know my game. I'm not a power hitter. I'm not an RBI guy. I just try and have good at-bats and get on base."** — **Infielder Marco Scutaro**

out of contention early and shipped him to the Giants in July for minor league second baseman Charlie Culberson.

Scutaro's new teammates shake their heads when describing his ability to make contact.

They're just as baffled by his inability to stick in one organization. Scutaro, a .273 career hitter, has played six positions in his career and is comfortable at either middle infield spot and at third base.

The problem isn't off the field.

Rockies manager Jim Tracy calls Scutaro "one of the classiest human beings I've ever had the privilege of being associated with." And Giants backup catcher and fellow Venezuelan Hector Sanchez simply calls him "The Captain."

"Everybody listens to Marco," Sanchez said. "He knows so much about baseball, and he'll help you all the time. You have to watch him, too. You learn from watching his at-bats."

Tracy said it was disappointing to let Scutaro go, partly because of how he was mentoring the Rockies' young players.

Scutaro's desire to help isn't limited to young teammates. When the Giants were in San Diego last month, Scutaro told Ryan Theriot, his primary competition at second base, that he thought Theriot could benefit from mechanical changes that Scutaro remembered from Theriot's time with the Chicago Cubs.

"That's who he is," Tracy said. "It's no coincidence that this guy shows up on winning teams."

Yet he keeps playing on new ones. Scutaro has twice been let go on waivers and has been traded four times, including July's swap that came about because the Giants

were looking for depth and a temporary replacement for Pablo Sandoval, who had just strained his hamstring.

"It's hard to believe this guy has traveled through (so many) teams to get to us," vice president of player operations Bobby Evans said. "He's just an all-around player. This has worked out well."

Scutaro, who hit .271 in 95 games with the Rockies, has upped his game down the stretch.

His at-bats have become must-see events for teammates, in large part because of what they hardly ever see. Scutaro has swung and missed just 6 percent of the time he's seen a strike this season.

From Aug. 10 to Sept. 3, Scutaro whiffed just twice. In a crucial three-game series against the Dodgers over the weekend, he swung and missed once.

It's the sign of a player who is comfortable at the plate, no matter what uniform he might be wearing.

"I don't mind the moves as long as I stay in the big leagues," Scutaro said. "It's kind of good to know that people want your services." ■

Giants infielder Marco Scutaro slides into third base during the fourth inning of Game 1 of the NLCS. (Nhat V. Meyer/Staff)

Melk Man's Spoils Leave a Sour Taste

Cabrera Receives 50-Game Suspension for PEDs

By Tim Kawakami

SAN FRANCISCO—Melky Cabrera's story was too good to be true, too tainted to pass a drug test and all too hauntingly familiar for a franchise cursed by steroids.

You thought the Giants and their fans would never go through the wringer with a star left fielder again?

You believed the joy and sunny good tidings of the 2010 World Series and the post-Barry Bonds era would last forever?

The answer was provided in sledgehammer form less than an hour before Wednesday's game at AT&T Park: No, the dark cloud is back over the Giants and everything they have achieved or might accomplish in 2012.

They harbored, and flourished with, a cheater, again.

On Wednesday, it was announced that Cabrera, this year's All-Star Game MVP and sterling new Giants addition, tested positive for testosterone and had been suspended 50 games, effective immediately.

The stunning news was followed by a 6-4 loss to the Washington Nationals that seemed depressingly fitting for the sellout crowd and all associated with the franchise.

"That is crushing, obviously, to hear that our best hitter's not going to be in the lineup," said Tim Lincecum, who started and lost the game. "But that's just like a day where they get a day off. So you've got to approach it that way."

Cabrera spoke to manager Bruce Bochy and general manager Brian Sabean after the ruling and acknowledged his guilt and offered his apologies in a statement.

After the game, his teammates suggested they would move beyond this as they have moved past key injuries; but the ripple effects are far greater than just an injury.

Practically, the Giants lost one of the league's best hitters (with an asterisk) for the rest of the regular season.

Symbolically, Cabrera's sudden fall was just another reminder that skepticism always legitimately surrounds the greatest sporting achievements. Especially in baseball and, unfortunately, often when it involves the Giants.

For the Giants and their fans, it's a harsh flashback to the Bonds days, when the home run king dominated the game while hearing accusations of steroid use.

In an incredible coincidence, Bonds himself was in attendance for Wednesday's game, leaving in the eighth inning to his regular rousing applause. And with the Giants losing.

Until Wednesday, Cabrera was having a career season no one could have imagined. Now, we have a sad explanation for it.

"We're disappointed," Bochy said after the game of Cabrera's suspension. "Melky was having a really nice year for us. But our thoughts are right now, we move on. That's all you can do.

"Whether it's an injury or something like this, this team will remain focused on trying to win ballgames and that's where we're at right now. That never changes. We've dealt with some things you have to handle and this is one of them. So that's our focus: Focus forward."

Cabrera was acquired in the winter from the Kansas City Royals for erratic pitcher Jonathan Sanchez, who has since been dropped and dispatched to the Colorado Rockies.

Cabrera had been a revelation for the Giants — one of the league's most reliable hitters, a strong thrower and a convivial personality in the clubhouse.

Now he's gone for the regular season, and it will be almost impossible for the Giants to fully replace him.

The Giants have to forge ahead. Gregor Blanco went into the outfield to replace Cabrera; newly acquired Hunter Pence can presumably replace some of the lost offense. ∎

Melky Cabrera collects his 50th hit in the month of May. The Giants left fielder was leading the National League in hitting when a positive test for testosterone in August resulted in a season-ending 50-game suspension. (Nhat V. Meyer/Staff)

#15
MANAGER
BRUCE BOCHY

Giants' Resilience Begins with Bochy

Alex Pavlovic • October 24, 2012

Dodgers manager Don Mattingly saw this coming a month ago. Mattingly, the captain of a sinking ship, looked across the field at the Giants dugout when the Dodgers visited AT&T Park in September. The Giants had withstood season-ending injuries to Brian Wilson and Freddy Sanchez, Melky Cabrera's suspension and the Dodgers' string of blockbuster deals.

And the resilient group was running away with the division.

"I don't think I ever expected them to stop performing the way they are because I've known Bruce Bochy for a long time," Mattingly said. "I know that the Giants are basically just going to keep coming at you. That's just typical Bruce Bochy.

"His teams are resilient. They never quit."

The never-say-die Giants are now champions of the National League and hosts of Wednesday's Game 1 of the World Series against the Detroit Tigers.

During a run that has included a record-tying six elimination-game victories, the Giants have seemingly taken their cues from Hunter Pence, who gives

raucous pregame speeches. But the Reverend Pence would like to let you in on a clubhouse secret.

"It actually starts at the top," Pence said. "There's a unique, relaxed and encouraging feeling that starts with Bochy. He's always calm, and that keeps us calm."

It wasn't always easy for Bochy to stay calm this season. The Giants were put through the wringer, starting with Wilson's elbow surgery in April. On Aug. 15, the Giants dealt with a bigger crisis when Cabrera, their All-Star No. 3 hitter, was suspended 50 games. Bochy met with the team, and long before players starting coming up with postseason mottos, he delivered one of his own: "Focus forward."

"As I've said many times," Bochy said. "It's not that it happens, it's how you deal with it."

Bochy has been dealing the same way for years, 18 of them, to be exact. Nearly two decades of managing will fill a résumé, and Bochy has. He ranks third among active managers with 1,454 wins and is tied for 14th all-time with six playoff appearances. A World Series win this season would be his second in three tries, giving the former catcher with a .239 career average a

Bruce Bochy watches batting practice before Game 7 of the National League Championship Series. In 18 years as a major league manager, Bochy has more than 1,400 career wins and two World Series rings. (Gary Reyes/Staff)

"**It actually starts at the top. There's a unique, relaxed and encouraging feeling that starts with Bochy. He's always calm, and that keeps us calm.**" — **Outfielder Hunter Pence**

reasonable argument to be a Hall of Famer.

Bochy won't be the one making the case.

"It's great when you hear good things," Bochy said. "The players would feel the same, but you can't believe all the good things or the bad things."

In quiet moments, Bochy concedes that he knows the criticism, mainly that he can be too loyal with veterans. But on one of the closest teams in recent Giants memory, the manager's loyalty is fiercely appreciated.

Tested by Tim Lincecum's surprising first-half slump, Bochy continually insisted that "this is still our guy." When Ryan Vogelsong slumped in August, Bochy ran the same play. "He's one of our guys," Bochy said after Vogelsong gave up seven runs in 3 ⅓ in mid-September. "I have all the confidence in the world in him."

That meant the world to the right-hander who traveled to Japan and Venezuela to resurrect his career.

"I've been on other side of this, where you're not hearing that," Vogelsong said. "He had my back, and it wasn't just publicly. After every start he would come and say: 'You're right there. Your stuff is good. You're on the brink of figuring it out.' That means a lot."

The manager's meetings were plentiful, and not just with veterans. When Brandon Crawford made a slew of errors in the season's opening weeks and struggled at the plate, Bochy called the 25-year-old shortstop into his office. The message was simple: Forget about your at-bats.

"He told me 'You're our shortstop. Just worry about playing good defense and you're going to be in the line-up every day,'" said Crawford, who recovered in the field and has been a postseason threat at the plate.

The message was a bit more complicated for the other young infielder. Brandon Belt hit .186 in July and went 1 for 20 on a road trip through Atlanta and Philadelphia that ended with Belt admitting that he was struggling with confidence.

Bochy gave Belt a couple days off to catch his breath.

"That helped tremendously," said Belt, who soon caught fire. "I needed to gather my thoughts, and he knew that."

Bochy isn't just pushing the right buttons off the field. He managed with urgency throughout the season, whether that meant using seven relief pitchers to get through three innings of an 8-3 September win over the Rockies, or using Sergio Romo to secure the final out of a 9-0 win in Game 7 of the NLCS.

In the first two rounds of the postseason, Bochy was continually a batter ahead of Cincinnati's Dusty Baker and St. Louis' Mike Matheny, both of whom left their winner-take-all starters in a touch too long.

The quick postseason thinking, first displayed during the 2010 championship run, doesn't surprise Bochy's players, who have found their 57-year-old manager to be adaptive off the field.

Bochy is a wine connoisseur and accompanies his wife to Broadway plays when the team visits New York, but he has little trouble identifying with players in an eclectic clubhouse that features a right fielder (Pence) who rides a scooter to the park, an injured pitcher (Wilson) who wears reflective shoes and a shutdown closer (Romo) who has piercings in his ears and a signature "That's what's up!" motto.

"He lets us be ourselves and do our thing," Romo said. "He's not judgmental at all. He had a lot of patience with us this season, which we needed.

"He let us come together as a team." ■

In six seasons as the Giants manager, Bruce Bochy has won more than 500 games and two World Series titles. (Jim Gensheimer/Staff)

#75
PITCHER

BARRY ZITO

Zito's Journey Is a Life Lesson

Monte Poole • October 24, 2012

In his hands was immense wealth, millions upon millions, enough to lavishly support several future generations. In his midst, surrounding his every move, were these constant omens of professional death.

Barry Zito was one of the richest poor souls on earth, a man with everything and a pitcher with nothing.

Yet Zito never surrendered or mentally checked out or got comfortable taking the paychecks he knew he hadn't earned. The left-hander kept searching for answers and seeking fulfillment, profoundly committed to giving his employers a return on the single biggest investment they'd ever made in an athlete.

And, finally, last week, there it was, Zito delivering the grittiest and most impressive performance of his career, inspiring and galvanizing the Giants, launching them past improbable odds and the St. Louis Cardinals.

"What he did in St. Louis," fellow starter Matt Cain said, "is something he needed. And something we really, really had to have."

The redemption of Zito is complete, at least in the eyes of his teammates and employers.

That the Giants are thanking Zito above all others, including NLCS MVP Marco Scutaro, for their presence on baseball's grandest stage, suggests something of a parable.

For Zito has spent much of his time in San Francisco being dismissed, if not booed off the field. He was deemed unworthy of a spot on the 2010 postseason roster, even though he owns the biggest contract in the building: $126 million over seven years, signed in 2007.

"It says a lot about his mental toughness, his make-up," manager Bruce Bochy said. "I mentioned this in 2010. It wasn't easy not to put him on the postseason (roster). He was struggling in September. But the way he handled it was so impressive. He went out, I think he threw a bullpen (session) that day. And throughout the postseason, he kept himself ready in case something happened."

After seven very good years in Oakland (102-63), Zito had become the biggest financial black hole in Giants history, entering 2012 with a 43-61 record in San Francisco.

Barry Zito pitches against the Tigers in Game 1 of the 2012 World Series. Zito signed a seven-year, $126 million contract before the 2007 season, but posted losing records in each of his first five seasons in a Giants uniform. In 2012, he rebounded to post a 15-8 record. (Nhat V. Meyer/Staff)

"I told him that 'I'm glad to hand you the ball for the first game,' with all he's been through and the way he's handled it. It's been off the charts." — Manager Bruce Bochy

So awful was Zito in spring training this year — 7.91 ERA, 44 base runners in 19 1/3 innings — that the Giants departed Arizona without him. He was left behind to, um, fine-tune his delivery mechanics.

When a pitcher is almost 34 and coming off five consecutive losing seasons, the last of which included an extended visit to Triple-A Fresno, being left at the minor league complex to work on your mechanics is a euphemism for trying to save your career.

Zito responded by actually adjusting his mechanics. Summoned to join the Giants in Colorado for an April 9 start, he responded with a four-hit shutout of the Rockies, giving San Francisco its first win of the season.

It was Zito's first shutout in a Giants uniform and the precursor to his best season with the team. He finished 15-8 with a 4.15 ERA.

"I feel like I've grown up in this game, you know?" Zito said. "When I came up in Oakland, I felt like I was a boy in the game. You have talent and you just keep going to the next level, and all of a sudden everyone is kind of like looking at you and there's fans chanting your name and stuff, and you're not really sure why."

Zito throughout his maturation has pitched himself off countless professional cliffs, tinkering with this, tampering with that. But he keeps climbing back up to the road, dusting himself off and getting back behind the wheel.

There is no more prestigious wheel than that which signifies starting Game 1 of a World Series.

"For him to keep grinding, as we say, and trying to get better, for him to be at this point and starting the first game, I was really glad, proud to tell him that," Bochy said. "And I told him that 'I'm glad to hand you the ball for the first game,' with all he's been through and the way he's handled it. It's been off the charts."

It's Zito's turn in the rotation, but he earned this Game 1 start. He's not the pitcher Bochy has to work around anymore, or the guy general manager Brian Sabean might consider the biggest impediment to a better roster.

Zito is the pitcher his teammates not only endorse to start Game 1 but extol as a man. It's almost as if they feel they owe him.

"If you look at Game 6 and Game 7 and break it down, Barry's game is what showed us how to win the next two," said Ryan Vogelsong, who followed Zito and won Game 6 against St. Louis.

That Zito would provide the pivotal performance, his masterpiece in the crucial Game 5 of the NLCS, is nothing short of lessons that can be applied to life.

Better to be defined not by the knockdowns but by the rising in response. And money always smells better when it's earned on merit. ∎

Barry Zito pitches against the Tigers in Game 1 of the World Series. Zito was one of baseball's top pitchers during his first seven major league seasons with the Athletics — winning the American League Cy Young award in 2002 and 102 games while in Oakland. (Nhat V. Meyer/Staff)

Getting It Done
'Relentless' Giants Capture N.L. West Crown

By Alex Pavlovic

SAN FRANCISCO—They came together despite crushing injuries and unexpected slumps. They stayed together through a spending spree by their closest rivals and a suspension that rocked baseball but only furthered the resolve within the clubhouse.

On Saturday, the Giants finally got to celebrate together.

An 8-4 victory over the San Diego Padres at AT&T Park clinched the organization's second National League West title in three years and set off a wild celebration for a team that brought in plenty of new faces this season but again found the right mix.

"Everything that happened makes it that much more special," manager Bruce Bochy said. "I know there had to be people in baseball that thought we were in trouble at times, but these guys were relentless.

"We did this the way you're supposed to, and that's by going out and winning it."

The Giants trailed the Los Angeles Dodgers by 7½ games May 28, but slowly chipped away. When their eighth National League West title came into view, the Giants started firing on all cylinders. With Bochy preaching the need to "take care of business every day," the Giants won six straight to clinch the West, improving to 43-23 since the All-Star break.

That second-half stretch included one attention-getting Dodgers deal after another, but the Giants never looked south. Instead, they quietly pulled away with a lineup that gets contributions from top to bottom and always followed the lead of catcher Buster Posey, who only increased his production after left fielder Melky Cabrera was suspended.

A revolving cast of stars stepped up on a nightly basis. Saturday's key contributors included Marco Scutaro, a trade deadline pickup who drove in three runs, young first baseman Brandon Belt (home run, three runs scored), and even pitcher Madison Bumgarner, who delivered an RBI single in the second inning.

The clinching victory gave the Giants a season-high 11-game lead in the division and was their third consecutive division-clinching win that came against the Padres, Bochy's previous team.

Bochy has remained patient throughout the season, especially in the down times. He insisted that his team was better than it was showing, and as the intensity picked up down the stretch, Bochy slowed things down, managing every game as if it were Game 7 of the World Series.

Bochy's players made his job a bit easier Saturday night. Sacrifice flies by Posey and Hunter Pence scored two runs in the first inning, and Bumgarner drove Belt in an inning later. Belt and shortstop Brandon Crawford reached base to lead off the fourth inning, and Scutaro's two-out, two-run single gave the Giants a 5-1 lead.

"He just never seems to be in a hurry," Posey said of Scutaro. "He's patiently aggressive, is how I would put it."

The Giants have been riding the hot streaks of Posey, Scutaro and others in recent weeks, and Saturday they improved to 15-5 in September.

"I can't remember a team that attacked the schedule at the end of the season like they did," general manager Brian Sabean said. "They love the game and respect the game, and they try to win every single inning.

"This is a special group." ■

Giants third baseman Pablo Sandoval hurdles the railing to catch a Yonder Alonso foul ball during the Giants' September 22 win over the San Diego Padres, which clinched the National League West crown. (Jim Gensheimer/Staff)

NATIONAL LEAGUE DIVISION SERIES: GAME 1
OCTOBER 6, 2012 | REDS 5, GIANTS 2

Missed Chance
Giants Can't Capitalize on Injury to Reds Ace

By Alex Pavlovic

> **It was a little bit of a curveball for both teams. But it's still going to be a grind."**
>
> — **Right fielder Hunter Pence**

SAN FRANCISCO—A Giants team that prides itself on resiliency was beaten at its own game Saturday night.

The Reds lost Game 1 starter Johnny Cueto after just eight pitches, but the Giants couldn't take advantage, losing 5-2 and falling behind in the best-of-five National League Division Series. Matt Cain gave up two big homers, and five Reds pitchers combined for 8 $^2/_3$ relief innings as Cincinnati stole a game at AT&T Park.

Cueto had trouble warming up and looked uncomfortable from the start. He retired just one hitter before being pulled with back spasms.

"When Johnny went down, I was like, 'Oh, man, we're done,'" Reds second baseman Brandon Phillips said. "'Why? Why?'"

The Giants found themselves asking, "How? How?"

How could they give this one back?

Instead of facing a fellow Cy Young Award candidate, Cain eventually squared off against Game 3 starter Mat Latos, who made his first career relief appearance. Latos lasted nearly as many innings as Cain did, giving up just a Buster Posey homer in four crucial relief innings.

After Cueto left, the Giants managed just one hit in 1 $^2/_3$ innings off immediate replacement Sam LeCure, who was followed by Latos.

"It was a little bit of a curveball for both teams," Giants right fielder Hunter Pence said. "But it's still going to be a grind."

Only one team found a way to grind out the rest of the night, and it wasn't the one that overcame a season-ending injury to its marquee closer and a 50-game suspension for its All-Star left fielder. Cain has been a guiding light in a season built on overcoming adversity, but his outing Saturday was a short one. ∎

Giants outfielder Gregor Blanco makes the last out during the eighth inning of Game 1 at AT&T Park. (Jim Gensheimer/Staff)

"We can bounce back. I've got all the faith in the world in us."

— Right fielder Hunter Pence

The Giants' ace entered the night with 21⅓ career scoreless innings in the postseason but was taken out after he gave up three runs on two homers in just five innings. Phillips hit a two-run shot on a hanging curveball in the third inning; Jay Bruce hit a blast to right in the fourth.

"That's just something that you don't want to happen in a big-game situation," Cain said. "The hanging breaking balls in these games always hurt a little bit more. I made some bad pitches and put these guys in a hole. That's my fault.

The Giants tried to hit their way out of the hole but never could quite find one. Cain had hit a bases-loaded shot to right in the second but had nothing to show for it. Pence twice thought he hit balls as well as possible but watched the shots die in the damp San Francisco air.

Pence reached on an error to lead off the fourth but was immediately doubled off when Brandon Belt scorched a shot right at first baseman Joey Votto.

"We had a tough night," manager Bochy said. "I thought we had better at-bats than what it looked like. We didn't have a lot of things going for us."

The Reds did, in a very unorthodox way.

Latos had thrown 78 pitches Tuesday and was scheduled to start this coming Tuesday, but he was rushed into duty and handled it with aplomb. A long-time Giants nemesis because of comments he made in 2010 while with the San Diego Padres, Latos handed a 3-1 lead to the traditional members of a bullpen that led the majors in ERA this season.

Still, the Giants had a chance.

Left-hander Sean Marshall set down the Giants in order in the seventh, but they got two runners on against Jonathan Broxton in the eighth. The former Los Angeles Dodgers closer went to a full count on Gregor Blanco before striking him out looking on a fastball that could have been called either way.

"I thought it was a little outside," Blanco said. "But the umpire makes a decision. It was a tough call for me, but it happens."

Against the odds, the Giants twice brought the tying run to the plate in the ninth. The Reds scored two in the top of the inning to hand a 5-1 lead to Aroldis Chapman, an All-Star closer who regularly touches triple digits.

But Chapman was wild, and he loaded the bases on a single and two walks. A wild pitch scored one, but Chapman retired Pablo Sandoval and struck out Posey swinging on 100 mph fastball.

"We can bounce back," Pence said. "I've got all the faith in the world in us."

The problem for the Giants: After overcoming a serious obstacle of their own Saturday on the road, the Reds feel the same way.

"This is a resilient team," Reds manager Dusty Baker said. "They can pick each other up and go on."

Only one team will, and at the moment, it's not the Giants in the driver's seat. ■

Opposite: Giants shortstop Brandon Crawford, pitcher Matt Cain and catcher Buster Posey huddle with pitching coach Dave Righetti (in jacket). Above: The Giants dugout looks on, hoping for a rally in Game 1. (Nhat V. Meyer/Staff)

NATIONAL LEAGUE DIVISION SERIES: GAME 2
OCTOBER 7, 2012 | REDS 9, GIANTS 0

Blowout Leaves Giants on Brink

S.F. Limited to Two Hits, One Loss Away From Offseason

By Alex Pavlovic

> **Honestly, I felt pretty good. They hit it where we weren't. That's what it seemed like."**
>
> — Pitcher
> **Madison Bumgarner**

SAN FRANCISCO—With Matt Cain and Madison Bumgarner opening a series at AT&T Park, many of the Giants felt they would be perfectly positioned to kick off another deep postseason run.

Two games in, the Giants are on the verge of elimination.

They looked flat and overmatched in a 9-0 loss to the Cincinnati Reds on Sunday night and now sit one loss from the offseason after the worst postseason shutout in franchise history.

"It's definitely disappointing," catcher Buster Posey said. "With as good as Cainer and Bum are, you definitely would have liked to get at least one game."

A night after Cain gave up three earned runs in five innings, Bumgarner

was charged with four in 4^1/$_3$. Bumgarner had a 2.38 ERA in 15 regular season starts at AT&T Park, but it was Bronson Arroyo who looked right at home on this night.

Arroyo needed just 91 pitches to get through seven one-hit innings. Brandon Belt broke up the perfect game with a two-out single in the fifth, but the Giants didn't have another base runner until the seventh, when Posey drew a two-out walk. Neither runner reached scoring position.

With Arroyo serving up a soft mix of changeups, sinkers and sweeping breaking balls, the Giants went 11 straight batters at one point without getting a ball out of the infield.

"He really kept us off balance," Belt said. "Those (soft throwers) are generally

Giants right fielder Hunter Pence (left) and catcher Buster Posey agonize over the team's Game 2 struggles. (Jim Gensheimer/Staff)

"
It's definitely disappointing. With as good as (Matt) Cainer and (Madison) Bum (Bumgarner) are, you definitely would have liked to get at least one game." — Catcher Buster Posey

hard to handle for big leaguers because it's such a change of pace."

Bumgarner's pace shifted dramatically in the second inning. In his first postseason appearance since a brilliant eight-inning outing in Game 4 of the 2010 World Series, Bumgarner at first looked headed for another gem. He struck out Zack Cozart and Joey Votto in the first inning and needed just 12 pitches to set down the Reds.

But Ryan Ludwick stunned Bumgarner by crushing a solo homer on a first-pitch fastball in the second inning.

The Reds kept the line moving in the fourth while scoring three more times. Votto hit a leadoff single, and Ludwick followed with a soft base hit. After a pop-up, Scott Rolen drove in a run with a single to right. Hunter Pence overthrew the cutoff man, allowing both runners to advance — both scored on Ryan Hanigan's single to center.

"Honestly, I felt pretty good," Bumgarner said. "They hit it where we weren't. That's what it seemed like."

Bumgarner wasn't the only one to feel that way. The Giants couldn't get a big hit to fall in Game 1 and couldn't find a hole early in Game 2 as the crowd grew restless. Needing someone to bring some life back to AT&T Park, manager Bruce Bochy called for Tim Lincecum in the sixth inning.

After some initial confusion as Bochy made a double-switch, Lincecum took the mound cold, fired just a handful of warm-up pitches, calmly tied the laces on his cleats and set about retiring the Reds in order.

For a moment, AT&T Park rocked, a sellout crowd urging the Giants to overcome what was then a four-run deficit.

"It felt like that might be the turning point," Posey said. "That's what you hope."

Instead, the Giants went down on just nine pitches in the bottom of the frame.

"It seems like every time we try and get something going, they just don't let us," second baseman Marco Scutaro said.

Scutaro and Angel Pagan were the spark plugs atop the lineup as the Giants cruised to an N.L. West title. But through two games they're just 1 for 17, and the Giants have just two runs on nine hits.

Scutaro ended the regular season with a 20-game hitting streak. But like the rest of the Giants, he has found the sledding much tougher in the postseason.

"Obviously, things haven't gone the way we expected," he said. "It seems like every ball they hit, hard or soft, it finds a hole. They're getting the big hits. Their momentum is really good right now."

The Giants need three straight road wins to keep their season alive. Bochy said he didn't need to deliver a special message after Sunday's blowout.

"We know where we're at right now," he said. "Our backs are to the wall."

Several Giants took solace in that they've been successful on the road this season and pointed out that a three-game run isn't out of the question.

"The plan is to go out there and do the same thing at their field that they did at ours," Belt said.

The Reds, now controlling every aspect of this series, did have four three-game losing streaks in the regular season.

But none of them came at home. ∎

Giants manager Bruce Bochy takes the ball from starter Madison Bumgarner. Bumgarner, who had thrown spectacularly during the 2010 World Series, allowed seven hits and four earned runs in $4^1/_3$ innings. (Jim Gensheimer/Staff)

NATIONAL LEAGUE DIVISION SERIES: GAME 3
OCTOBER 9, 2012 | GIANTS 2, REDS 1, 10 INNINGS

Emotional Win for Giants

Pence's Speech, Vogelsong's Grit Prove Inspiring

By Alex Pavlovic

> **We want to play more baseball — together. This win was the embodiment of 'team.' Everyone came together."**
>
> — **Right fielder Hunter Pence**

CINCINNATI—The most emotional day of the Giants' season ended with pure, unadulterated joy.

Buster Posey scored the go-ahead run on an error in the top of the 10th inning at Great American Ball Park as the Giants fought to a 2-1 victory Tuesday over the Cincinnati Reds. The Giants trail 2-1 in the best-of-five National League Division Series after beating a team that again had a starting pitcher flirt with a no-hitter.

The seeds for victory were planted during an intense pregame meeting that several players said was more apt of a football locker room. Hunter Pence, who later contributed to the winning run while fighting through a calf cramp, gave a fiery speech to a team that came to Cincinnati needing three victories to keep its season alive.

"It really touched home," starting pitcher Ryan Vogelsong said. "It wasn't what he said, it was the intensity of it. The truth of it."

The new truth for the Giants is that they are more than just alive. As the banged-up Reds scrambled to find a Game 4 starter, the Giants stood defiantly in the visiting clubhouse, vowing to bring the same fight Wednesday.

"We want to play more baseball — together," Pence said. "This win was the embodiment of 'team.' Everyone came together."

Whereas Pence led the pregame charge, Vogelsong did the heavy lifting once the

Giants right fielder Hunter Pence, a mid-season pickup from the Philadelphia Phillies, celebrates the win with fellow outfielders Gregor Blanco and Angel Pagan. (Gary Reyes/Staff)

lights went on. A night earlier, he had received a text message from friend Jamie Moyer, who has been pitching in the big leagues since Vogelsong was a child.

Moyer recapped Vogelsong's fairy-tale path from journeyman to All-Star and told him, "I know you've been waiting a long time for this. Just go get it done."

Vogelsong more than held his own, keeping pace with Homer Bailey for five innings even as the Reds starter bid for his second no-hitter in three starts. Vogelsong's night wasn't easy at first; the Reds had three hits and a walk in the first inning but scored just one run, in large part because Brandon Phillips ran into an out at third base.

Vogelsong got a second Pence push in the second inning, when the right fielder crashed into the wall in foul territory while making a sliding catch. They met in the dugout, and this time Vogelsong was the one doing the talking.

"I told him, 'You don't know how much that play did for me,'" Vogelsong said. "And I really didn't need much motivation because this was my first postseason start."

Calm and locked in after Pence's catch, Vogelsong cruised through the fifth inning. He allowed just two more base runners before being lifted for a pinch hitter.

After the win, Vogelsong's voice cracked as he tried to put his first postseason experience into words.

"I've been waiting for this moment a long time," he said.

Manager Bruce Bochy said Vogelsong "saved" the rest of the Giants as they tried to get settled in, and it took quite a while. The Giants had tied the game in the third inning on a hit batsman, a walk and two sacrifices, but Bailey owned the stage for the next four innings. He struck out six straight at one point and finished with a Reds postseason record 10 strikeouts.

Two nights after Bronson Arroyo pitched seven innings of one-hit ball in Game 2, Bailey did the same, allowing just a Marco Scutaro single with two outs in the sixth inning. Bailey became just the fourth pitcher in postseason history to throw seven innings, allow one

hit and strike out 10, but he didn't leave with a lead, thanks to Vogelsong.

"Yeah, I knew he was throwing a no-hitter," Vogelsong said. "I also knew I had to put up zeros and keep us right there."

Pence, praised by Vogelsong, volleyed it back in his direction. "He was enormous," Pence said. "He kept getting us back (in the dugout). Kept getting us back in there."

Still, the Giants at first looked hapless against the Reds bullpen. In all, the Giants struck out 16 times, the most in a postseason game since 2005.

But Posey got them going in the 10th with a leadoff single against Jonathan Broxton. Pence had cramped up in Game 2 and did so again in the middle of his at-bat against Broxton. But with just one position player left on the bench, he stayed in the game and knocked a base hit into left. It was the first hit of the series for Pence, who said he would be able to start Game 4.

"Maybe (the cramp) helped my at-bat," Pence said, smiling. "I couldn't move my legs."

He hobbled to first and then moved no farther for two at-bats as Brandon Belt and Xavier Nady struck out. With Joaquin Arias at the plate, a passed ball advanced Poscy and Pence. Arias hit a 1-2 fastball to third and put his head down, not knowing Scott Rolen had bobbled the grounder. He beat the throw to first as Posey scored the run that gave the Giants the lead — their first of the series.

"I think we have to be really happy that we came away with this win tonight," Posey said, "Because we didn't swing the bats very well at all."

The Giants were all smiles as highlights of the win played in a clubhouse where the players had stood hours earlier, listening as Pence delivered a message to "keep pushing, keep pushing."

The Giants were happy, but they weren't satisfied.

"We came here to win three games in a row," center fielder Angel Pagan said. "We didn't come here to win one game." ■

Giants third baseman Pablo Sandoval, who missed much of the season due to injury, reacts after striking out in the first inning. (Patrick Tehan/Staff)

NATIONAL LEAGUE DIVISION SERIES: GAME 4

OCTOBER 10, 2012 | GIANTS 8, REDS 3

Giants Change for the Better

Offense Gets Going, Giving S.F. Confidence

By Alex Pavlovic

> **When you're on a stage like this, you're hoping somebody steps up. Timmy (Lincecum) has that ability, and he did tonight.**
>
> — Manager Bruce Bochy

CINCINNATI—The new slogan for the Giants' 2012 postseason isn't particularly good for the health, or clubhouse ambience, but it's effective.

After Wednesday's 8-3 win over the Cincinnati Reds that forced a winner-take-all Game 5 in the National League Division Series, Tim Lincecum turned to a group of smiling teammates.

"Same clothes tomorrow!" he yelled.

The Giants don't intend to make any off-field changes Thursday as they aim to become the first team in League Division Series history to overcome a 2-0 deficit by winning three straight games on the road. Players must wear the same street clothes (although they're allowed to swap in a new pair of underwear), and Hunter Pence will give the same fiery speech that he has given before both victories at Great American Ball Park.

On the field, however, the Giants have morphed by leaps and bounds since falling behind with two lackluster efforts in San Francisco.

A night after becoming the first team in eight years to win a postseason game with fewer than four hits, the Giants had 11 hits, including homers from Angel Pagan, Gregor Blanco and Pablo Sandoval.

And Lincecum, long the mainstay of the rotation, came out of the bullpen firing strikes. Left out of the postseason rotation, Lincecum earned the win with $4\frac{1}{3}$ dominant innings in relief of Barry Zito, who was knocked out in the third.

Giants pitcher Tim Lincecum, a two-time Cy Young Award winner, came out of the bullpen to help the Giants win Game 4. (Patrick Tehan/Staff)

"He's a big-game pitcher, a big-time pitcher," Pence said of Lincecum. "We always believed in him."

Through three games, it was hard to believe the Giants would hit enough to overcome a deep Reds team. The Giants had just four runs in the first three games of the series and were hitting .126 as a team.

Pagan, a catalyst during the second-half surge, put a charge into the dugout with a solo homer off Mike Leake two pitches into the game. The laser shot was the first postseason leadoff homer in the franchise's history.

"He woke up the offense," Sandoval said.

Did he ever.

Blanco hit a two-run shot in the second inning, his first homer since July 18. The blast gave Zito a cushion to work with, but he couldn't find his way. Zito gave up a hit and walked three in the first inning but allowed just one run. After escaping another jam in the second inning, he gave up a solo homer to Ryan Ludwick in the third. A two-out walk later in the inning ended Zito's first postseason appearance with the Giants after just eight outs.

Zito was charged with two runs on four walks and four hits.

"I was just trying to be too fine, and it was a frustrating situation," Zito said. "Sometimes you want it so badly, but you have to remember to stay with each pitch."

Zito wasn't frustrated after the game, in large part because of what happened right after he exited. George Kontos got the Giants out of the third inning, and when the Reds got two runners on with one out in the fourth, Jose Mijares came in and struck out Reds No. 3 hitter Joey Votto. With Ludwick looming, manager Bruce Bochy called Lincecum in for his second relief appearance in three games.

"When you're on a stage like this, you're hoping somebody steps up," Bochy said. "Timmy has that ability, and he did tonight."

Lincecum struck out Ludwick, flicking the switch on his most electric performance of the season.

He pitched 4$^1/_3$ innings, the longest postseason relief outing by a Giant since Kirk Rueter went the same distance in the 2000 NLDS. Lincecum struck out six and allowed just one run as the Giants pulled away, with Sandoval's mammoth two-run blast in the seventh being the big blow. In two relief appearances this series, Lincecum has thrown 6$^1/_3$ innings and given up just three hits and an earned run while striking out eight.

"You're just here to get outs until they tell you you're done," Lincecum said. "You kind of go out there with that expectation of doing well, and when things go well, you think this is the way it should be."

Lincecum's teammates felt the same way. Asked what he expected when No. 55 came running out of the bullpen, Buster Posey smiled.

"That," he said emphatically. "What he did. I think that everybody on the team expects that."

The Giants, with their offense finally in gear and their bullpen rested thanks to Lincecum's long outing, have high expectations for Thursday. Only seven teams in history have come back from a 0-2 deficit to win a best-of-five postseason series. None has done what the Giants will attempt to do Thursday, when they aim to sweep all three games at the home of the National League Central champion Reds.

"We weren't thinking about three games when we came here," Sandoval said. "We've been going day by day, game by game."

The Giants and Reds are down to one day and one game: Matt Cain versus Mat Latos. It's all hands on deck, and even Lincecum said he would be available after throwing 55 pitches, 42 of them for strikes. He promised to wear the same maroon T-shirt, and said he's looking forward to Pence's third speech in three days.

"Oh yeah, I've got one more of those," Pence said before pausing and flashing a mischievous smile. "Actually, I've got a lot more of those, hopefully." ■

Giants shortstop Brandon Crawford (left) high-fives right fielder Gregor Blanco after Blanco's second inning home run in Game 3. (Patrick Tehan/Staff)

NATIONAL LEAGUE DIVISION SERIES: GAME 5
OCTOBER 11, 2012 | GIANTS 6, REDS 4

One More for the Road

Posey's Grand Slam Put Giants into History Books

By Alex Pavlovic

> "You can't let that ball get past you. I was going to block that with my teeth if I had to."
>
> — Center fielder Angel Pagan

CINCINNATI—A third straight road victory over the Cincinnati Reds that transformed the Giants' season from improbable to historic also left closer Sergio Romo drenched, exhausted and emotional.

As his teammates celebrated a 6-4 series-clinching win Thursday, Romo stood in a corner of the clubhouse, hands on bent knees, eyes welled with tears. He had given every ounce of himself with a 35-pitch save, and the magnitude of the moment hit him.

The Giants had just become the first team in Major League Baseball history to wipe out a two-game deficit in a best-of-five series by winning three straight on the road, and Romo had sealed the deal. He got four outs, including a fly out to end an epic 12-pitch battle with Jay Bruce, who represented the winning run in the ninth inning.

"I'm just very proud to be the guy they asked to get that last out," Romo said softly. "I couldn't let them down. It's easy to be emotional about things like this because it's good emotion."

The Giants have been riding positive emotions since they stepped into the Reds' home park. It started with Hunter Pence's speech on Tuesday, which became a pregame ritual when the Giants won in extra innings that night to stave off elimination. The message always is a simple one: "Let's give ourselves another day together, another game together."

Behind Romo's heroics, Matt Cain's resilience and Buster Posey's monster

Giants catcher Buster Posey hits a grand slam in the fifth inning, swinging momentum toward the Giants. (Gary Reyes/Staff)

grand slam, the Giants clinched at least four more games together. They advanced to the National League Championship Series for the second time in three years and will face the St. Louis Cardinals.

Posey provided the decisive blast, a fifth-inning grand slam off Mat Latos to give the longtime Giants foe another reason to continue signing baseballs with the phrase "I hate SF!"

San Francisco couldn't possibly have more love for Posey, who displayed a rare bit of bravado after crushing a 2-2 fastball from Latos. He watched the ball soar 434 feet into the left-field stands as Latos and Reds catcher Ryan Hanigan walked in the other direction, suddenly trailing 6-0.

"This is probably right behind the World Series win," a smiling Posey said of the three-game comeback tour.

The Giants have always struggled to hit Latos, who had a 2.19 ERA in 11 career starts against them and pitched four strong relief innings in Game 1. But Gregor Blanco drew first blood in the fifth inning, lining a single and scoring on Brandon Crawford's triple, his first career postseason hit.

Crawford scored on an error and the Giants loaded the bases ahead of Posey, who at 25 already has a résumé that includes a World Series title, Rookie of the Year award, and possibly soon, a selection as MVP.

He added to the list Thursday. Posey joined Chuck Hiller (1962) and Will Clark (1989) as the only players in franchise history to hit a postseason grand slam. Yogi Berra (1956) and Eddie Perez (1998) were the only previous catchers in MLB history to have hit one in the playoffs.

"I was happy to come up in that situation," Posey said. "Those are the types of spots you work really hard for and try to enjoy."

Even with a six-run lead, the Giants weren't able to enjoy the next three innings. The Reds kept pushing, but each time were knocked back by a stellar defensive play by the Giants. Posey capped a huge sixth-inning strikeout of Hanigan by throwing Bruce out as he attempted to steal third.

Manager Bruce Bochy said he had just one tough lineup decision to make before the winner-take-all game, and he stuck with his gut and Crawford, one of the best defensive shortstops in the game. Crawford rewarded that faith not only with the triple but also with a diving catch to rob Hanigan with a runner on in the eighth.

The Reds brought the tying run to the plate in the final four innings, and when they threatened in the eighth, Bochy called for Romo. His first opponent, Dioner Navarro, hit a sinking liner to center field but Angel Pagan made a spectacular sliding catch to end the inning.

"You can't let that ball get past you," Pagan said. "I was going to block that with my teeth if I had to."

Romo used different parts of his body when he came on for the tense ninth.

"You saw guts," Pence said.

"He's all heart," Pagan added.

Said George Kontos, who himself got a big out in the sixth, "Romo, he pitched his butt off."

Romo walked one and gave up two singles as the Reds inched closer in the ninth. Bruce wouldn't give in with two runners on, fouling off nine pitches.

"He had the same attitude as me: 'This guy is not going to beat me,'" Romo said.

Romo won the showdown.

Bruce flied out to left field, and a strikeout of Scott Rolen sealed the win for the Giants, the eighth team in history to come back from a two-game deficit in a five-game series.

"Look at my teammates," Romo said afterward. "Look how happy they are."

Around him, anyone with a jersey on was showered with champagne. Hugs were exchanged and teammates reminded each other that they had vowed not to change street clothes as long as they keep winning.

"We'll go series-to-series with that," Kontos said.

Behind him was a white board adorned with a short message that the Giants saw every time they took the field: "Everything you've got for the man beside you." ∎

Giants center fielder Angel Pagan makes a sliding catch during the eighth inning. (Gary Reyes/Staff)

The Giants celebrate their impressive come-from-behind victory. San Francisco rallied after losing the first two games at home, winning three straight in Cincinnati to take the National League Division Series. (Patrick Tehan/Staff)

NATIONAL LEAGUE CHAMPIONSHIP SERIES: GAME 1
OCTOBER 14, 2012 | CARDINALS 6, GIANTS 4

One for the Birds

Giants Again Dig Hole at the Start

By Alex Pavlovic

> **There's not a whole lot of life on the ball. It's been a few starts now where my stuff just hasn't been there."**
>
> **— Pitcher
> Madison Bumgarner**

SAN FRANCISCO—The Giants felt right at home Sunday, both in terms of location and circumstance.

After a 6-4 loss to the St. Louis Cardinals in Game 1 of the National League Championship Series, the Giants once again trail a series that started at home. They're 0-3 at home and 3-0 on the road in the postseason, and have yet to hold a lead in 27 innings at a raucous AT&T Park.

"You don't necessarily want to have your back against the wall all that much," first baseman Brandon Belt said.

Again, the starting pitcher left the rest of the Giants with little choice.

In the first Game 1 in LCS history in which both starters failed to make it past the fourth inning, Madison Bumgarner dug the deeper hole. He was charged with six earned runs on eight hits in 3²/₃ innings and in two postseason starts has given up 15 hits and 10 earned runs in just eight innings.

Through six postseason games, the Giants still have not had a starter go more than 5²/₃ innings. The four postseason starters — Bumgarner, Matt Cain, Ryan Vogelsong and Barry Zito — have a combined ERA of 6.55.

"They just can't put it together," catcher Buster Posey said. "I think it's a little surprising, but I don't think it's anything they can't turn around."

Bumgarner might not get a shot to do so. Manager Bruce Bochy wouldn't commit to Bumgarner as a Game 5 starter, saying the coaching staff would have to discuss his role from here on out.

A demotion wouldn't surprise Bumgarner, who said he would back any decision Bochy makes. Bumgarner insists he is healthy and mechanically sound but acknowledged that something is wrong.

"There's not a whole lot of life on the

Giants catcher Hector Sanchez hits a ball off his foot during Game 1 of the National League Championship Series. (Susan Tripp Pollard/Staff)

"We can't get ourselves behind the 8-ball. It was tremendous that we did it once. I think it would be asking a lot for us to do it again." — Pitcher Ryan Vogelsong

ball," Bumgarner said. "It's been a few starts now where my stuff just hasn't been there."

For Bumgarner, home used to be where he found solutions. He has a 3.08 ERA in 41 career regular-season starts at AT&T Park, but it was clear Sunday that this was a different Bumgarner.

He gave up a two-run homer to David Freese in the second inning and by the fourth inning was sitting at 89 mph with his fastball, two ticks below his normal velocity.

Against the Cincinnati Reds a week before, Bumgarner had three inconsistent innings before imploding in the fourth. The process repeated itself Sunday against the Cardinals.

Bumgarner gave up back-to-back doubles to Daniel Descalso and Pete Kozma with one out in the fourth and fell behind 4-0 when Jon Jay looped an RBI single into center field. Carlos Beltran broke the game open with a two-run homer, crushing a two-strike cutter that found too much of the plate.

"He's just struggling with his command," Posey said. "His breaking balls are not getting buried in, and he doesn't have quite the same finish."

The Giants bullpen, on the other hand, had plenty of finish. Sparked by Tim Lincecum, the bullpen threw 5⅓ hitless innings, tying a postseason record and setting an LCS mark.

The Cardinals bullpen was more than capable of keeping pace, and they were forced to.

After Bumgarner was knocked out in the fourth, the Giants immediately rallied for four runs off Lance Lynn. Belt's single to center drove in the first Giants run at home in 13 innings, and Gregor Blanco followed with a two-run triple. Brandon Crawford's RBI double cut the deficit to two, and Lynn's night ended a batter later

when he walked pinch hitter Aubrey Huff.

"That all happened pretty fast," Cardinals manager Mike Matheny said. "They've got an explosive offense and made a strong run."

The run screeched to a halt when second baseman and Bay Area native Daniel Descalso made a diving stop on Angel Pagan's grounder.

"He made a great play," Pagan said. "I was just hoping that would get through."

Pagan and the rest of the Giants soon learned a valuable lesson: If you don't get to the Cardinals' starter, you might not get to the staff at all.

The Cardinals tied an NLCS record by using six relief pitchers in a nine-inning game, and nearly every one of them lit up the radar gun. Trevor Rosenthal comfortably pounded the strike zone with a slew of 99 mph fastballs, and after Edward Mujica struck out the side in the seventh, Mitchell Boggs and Jason Motte pumped 98 mph fastballs while getting through the final two innings.

"That's why we need a lead from the start," Pagan said. "Maybe then we won't have to face the nasty guys."

The Giants will turn to Vogelsong on Monday in an effort to finally grab a lead in a home game. Vogelsong gave up one run in five innings in a first-round start and said he feeds off the energy of a crowd that has sold out two straight seasons at AT&T Park.

Sparked in part by Vogelsong, the Giants overcame two home losses to the Reds in the National League Division Series. But against a team as resilient as the Cardinals, that might be an impossible task.

"We can't get ourselves behind the 8-ball," Vogelsong said. "It was tremendous that we did it once. I think it would be asking a lot for us to do it again." ∎

Giants third baseman Pablo Sandoval watches as the Cardinals' Daniel Descalso rounds third base to score on a Pete Kozma fourth-inning double. (Nhat V. Meyer/Staff)

NATIONAL LEAGUE CHAMPIONSHIP SERIES: GAME 2
OCTOBER 15, 2012 | GIANTS 7, CARDINALS 1

Giants Get Even
Vogelsong Delivers a Needed Strong Start

By Alex Pavlovic

Vogey really put us on his back tonight. It was big to get this one, really big."

— **Right fielder Hunter Pence**

SAN FRANCISCO—To keep themselves out of another tough situation, the Giants turned to two of their toughest players.

Starting pitcher Ryan Vogelsong delivered one of the best efforts of his career in the biggest game of his career, leading the Giants to a 7-1 victory over the St. Louis Cardinals that evened the National League Championship Series at 1-1 and kept them from having to overcome another deep series deficit. Marco Scutaro delivered the big hit, a bases-loaded single that knocked the Cardinals out three innings after he had nearly been knocked out of the game.

A hard and late slide at second base by Matt Holliday injured Scutaro's left hip in the first inning, and Scutaro was removed before the sixth inning to have X-rays taken. The test came back negative, but Scutaro will have an MRI exam, and his status for Game 3 is in doubt.

"I really think he got away with an illegal slide there," manager Bruce Bochy said of Holliday. "Marco was behind the bag and got smoked. It's a shame somebody got hurt because of this."

Vogelsong saw Scutaro walk gingerly back to his position after the collision and realized the onus was back on him.

"I felt like I really needed to make a pitch to the next guy to get him off the field," Vogelsong said. "You know he's not coming out of the game, whether he's really hurt or not. I just really was trying to make the next pitch to get the guy out so we could get (Scutaro) in the dugout."

Vogelsong induced a grounder that got the Giants out of the jam and Scutaro back to the team trainers. But that wasn't Vogelsong's biggest pitch of the night.

After a shaky start, he felt "something click mechanically" on a third-inning pitch.

"It was like, 'That's it right there —

Pitcher Sergio Romo celebrates after recording the last out of the Giants' 7-1 win in Game 2. (Nhat V. Meyer/Staff)

"What he did was extremely inspirational. (Marco) Scutaro pushing through there really pumped us up." — Right fielder Hunter Pence

that's how I want to feel,'" Vogelsong said. "That happens for me from time to time. I was able to sustain it and run with it."

The Giants hope Vogelsong can run with that feeling for a couple more weeks. And they hope the rest of the rotation can keep stride.

Vogelsong became the first Giants starter in seven postseason games to complete six innings and then went one more. He gave up four hits and one run while earning his first career postseason victory.

Vogelsong called it the best effort of a remarkable career that took him from Japan to the All-Star game in a span of two years. The win kept the Giants from having to overcome another 0-2 deficit on the road, a feat that most players agreed would have been all but impossible to pull off a second time.

"Vogey really put us on his back tonight," right fielder Hunter Pence said. "It was big to get this one, really big."

Vogelsong got the Giants off the field three pitches after Scutaro was knocked down, and Angel Pagan immediately kept the momentum going. Pagan hit a leadoff homer to right to give the Giants their first lead in a home game this postseason and make Pagan the second major leaguer to hit two leadoff homers in one postseason.

Pagan said he was angry after the top of the first inning, not at Holliday, who conceded the slide was late, but at the fact that the Giants' No. 2 hitter was ailing.

"You get angry to lose a player like Scutaro," Pagan said. "He's a huge piece of the puzzle."

Scutaro's teammates kept filling in new pieces as the Giants pulled away. Brandon Belt got the Giants going in the fourth with a one-out double that dropped into left field after nicking the end of his bat. Gregor Blanco chopped a high hopper over leaping third

baseman David Freese to send Belt to third. Brandon Crawford's slow roller was thrown away by pitcher Chris Carpenter as the Giants took a 2-1 lead.

"This is the playoffs," Belt said. "We don't care how it's done."

A walk to Pagan loaded the bases for Scutaro. He lined a sinker into left field, easily scoring Blanco and Crawford. Pagan raced home when the ball got past Holliday in left field.

"What he did was extremely inspirational," said Pence, the man who gives fiery speeches before every playoff game. "Scutaro pushing through there really pumped us up."

Scutaro's rebuttal gave the Giants a 5-1 lead, plenty on a day when Vogelsong was at his best. The other three starting pitchers in the postseason have given up 18 earned runs in $21^1/_3$ innings; Vogelsong has a 1.29 ERA in two postseason starts.

On a night when one of the Giants' most important players went down on a borderline dirty play, Vogelsong helped the Giants get revenge in their own way.

"The best thing is to just go out and do what we did tonight," catcher Buster Posey said. "Win a ball game." ■

Angel Pagan salutes the Giants dugout as he rounds third base following his leadoff home run. (Nhat V. Meyer/Staff)

NATIONAL LEAGUE CHAMPIONSHIP SERIES: GAME 3
OCTOBER 17, 2012 | CARDINALS 3, GIANTS 1

Hard Day's Night

Cain's Best Outing This Postseason Goes to Waste

By Alex Pavlovic

> **We missed some opportunities. We just weren't able to get that big hit. (Matt) Cain definitely threw the ball well enough to win."**
>
> **— Catcher Buster Posey**

ST. LOUIS—The stage was bigger and the stakes much higher, but the result was one Matt Cain and the Giants used to know well.

Cain showed up, the offense did not, and the Giants lost. A 3-1 setback Wednesday to the St. Louis Cardinals in a rain-delayed Game 3 put the Giants back a game in the best of seven National League Championship Series.

"He gave us a chance to win," manager Bruce Bochy said. "We had our chances."

Did they ever.

The Giants put multiple runners on base in six of the first seven innings but scored just one run off Kyle Lohse, who gave up seven hits and walked five. The Giants were 0 for 7 with runners in scoring position and left 11 runners on base. The game was delayed for three hours and 28 minutes in the seventh inning, leaving the position players with little to do but sit around and think about the first seven innings.

There wasn't much to be happy about.

Lohse walked two in the second but struck out Cain to end the inning. The Giants opened the third with an Angel Pagan single and Marco Scutaro double and took a 1-0 lead when Pablo Sandoval grounded out to short. But after an intentional walk to Buster Posey, Hunter Pence hit into a rally-killing double play.

The Giants left two more runners on base in the fourth, and Pence quieted another threat in the fifth by grounding out with Posey on base. Sandoval had already hit into a double play to wipe out Scutaro's single.

The theme continued in the sixth as the sky began to get dark and a wicked storm approached. Brandon Crawford and Cain hit two-out singles, but Pagan grounded out to short. After one-out singles by Sandoval

Giants pitcher Matt Cain reacts after streaking out with two men on base to end the second inning. The Giants stranded 11 base runners in the loss. (Gary Reyes/Staff)

" **I'm the goat today. I didn't get the job done in big opportunities. I've got to go home and learn from what happened and come back."** — Right fielder Hunter Pence

and Posey in the seventh, Pence struck out swinging and Brandon Belt struck out looking.

"We missed some opportunities," Posey said. "We just weren't able to get that big hit. Cain definitely threw the ball well enough to win."

The Giants didn't just waste endless golden opportunities to score. They wasted Cain's best effort of the postseason. Cain, long accustomed to unsupported quality starts, whiffed on his own opportunity in the third.

Carlos Beltran had exited after one inning with a left knee strain and was replaced by rookie Matt Carpenter, who came up with a runner on in the third. Carpenter was 4 for 4 previously off Cain but fell behind 0-2. When Cain grooved a 2-2 slider, Carpenter crushed it 428 feet into the right field stands.

"It was a slider down and in, and it didn't get in there like it should have," Cain said. "I made a bad pitch and it cost us. With (Beltran) out of the game, yeah, that's something you try to take advantage of.

"I didn't do it."

The homer was the first career postseason extra-base hit for Carpenter, who has six career homers.

"Really, I was just trying not to strike out," Carpenter said.

Pence had the opposite approach in his big moments, saying he tried to do too much. It cost the Giants. The No. 5 hitter was 0 for 4 — dropping his postseason average to .161 — and left five runners on base.

"I'm the goat today," Pence said. "I didn't get the job done in big opportunities. I've got to go home and learn from what happened and come back."

Posey, who has walked six times ahead of Pence this postseason, spread the blame around.

"He's definitely not the goat," Posey said. "I know I feel confidence every time he's up there with guys in scoring position. It's never on one guy."

Pence, Posey and the rest lamented their missed opportunities with runners in scoring position on a day that Cain called his best of the postseason. They failed to take advantage of one other break, too.

The Cardinals had scored a run in the seventh and threatened for more when the game was delayed just as Cain was pulled. After the long delay, Javier Lopez entered and quickly got the Giants out of the jam.

The break had served a huge benefit for the Giants, getting Mitchell Boggs — who struck out the only two Giants he faced — out of the game before the teams hit the eighth inning. With few appealing options, Cardinals manager Mike Matheny asked closer Jason Motte to get his first career six-out save.

"I was a little surprised he pitched the eighth," Posey said. "That's not easy to do."

The Giants made it a bit easier, going down on just nine pitches in the eighth inning. Motte needed only 10 pitches to get through the ninth, again setting the Giants down in order and preventing Posey from getting a final at-bat.

"Hopefully we don't have to get there," Pagan said of the back of the Cardinals' stellar bullpen. "Hopefully we get runs earlier."

Given every opportunity to do so Wednesday, the Giants couldn't get it done. ■

Giants outfielder Gregor Blanco breaks his bat in the sixth inning. The Giants outfielder was 0-for-3 in the loss. (Gary Reyes/Staff)

NATIONAL LEAGUE CHAMPIONSHIP SERIES: GAME 4
OCTOBER 18, 2012 | CARDINALS 8, GIANTS 3

No Time to Talk

Wainwright Sends S.F. to the Brink

By Alex Pavlovic

It's extremely disappointing just because you feel like you can pick your team up in a situation like this. But when you don't go and do it, it's that much harder of a fall."

— Pitcher Tim Lincecum

ST. LOUIS—The Giants don't need another fiery speech, another raucous dugout huddle or another round of mottos. After an 8-3 loss to the St. Louis Cardinals, the plan is simple: Find a way to score a few more runs or go home for the winter.

The lineup sputtered for the second straight game on Thursday at Busch Stadium as the Giants fell behind 3-1 in the best-of-seven National League Championship Series. The Giants have had their backs against the wall before, but the team that couldn't touch Adam Wainwright on Thursday looks much different from the one that scored 16 runs in the final three games against the Cincinnati Reds while streaking to a historic comeback.

"We just couldn't create anything today," leadoff hitter Angel Pagan said. "We've got to get something going. Today and yesterday, they were doing a really good job. They were keeping us off balance and staying in the zone."

The Giants offense showed signs of life just twice Thursday. Hunter Pence, who was moved down a spot in the lineup, hit a mammoth homer in the second inning. Pablo Sandoval hit a two-run shot in the ninth, long after Tim Lincecum exited his first start of the postseason.

Lincecum had given up just three hits and one run in 8 $\frac{1}{3}$ relief innings but couldn't keep that form in his return to a starting role. He struggled with fastball command and was knocked out in the fifth inning after giving up four runs on six hits and three walks.

"It's extremely disappointing just because you feel like you can pick your team up in a situation like this," Lincecum said. "But when you don't go and do it, it's that much harder of a fall, I guess."

The Cardinals got to Lincecum right

Third baseman Pablo Sandoval was unable to make a throw to first in the seventh inning. The Cardinals scored two runs in the inning to take an 8-1 lead. (Nhat V. Meyer/Staff)

"(Barry) Zito has been tremendous for us. We've got to find a way to get a win tomorrow, and if we go home to (Ryan) Vogelsong and (Matt) Cain throwing, we'll feel pretty good."

— Right fielder Hunter Pence

away, scoring two runs in a first inning that included three singles, a four-pitch walk and a couple hard-hit outs. Lincecum escaped further damage in the second inning when Matt Holliday's deep fly to left died on the warning track, and he retired the next seven Cardinals.

But the wheels came off again in the fifth.

Matt Carpenter, playing for injured right fielder Carlos Beltran, hit a one-out double. Holliday lined a single to center that was knocked down by a diving Angel Pagan, who made a quick throw to cutoff man Brandon Crawford. The shortstop one-hopped a throw to the plate that Hector Sanchez dropped, allowing Carpenter to score.

"I knew I had to be quick, because I knew he was going home," Crawford said. "I tried to give him the long hop. If I could do it again, I would hit him in the chest."

An RBI single by Yadier Molina scored Holliday and chased Lincecum.

"To get him out of the game was big for us," Holliday said. "Beating Tim Lincecum is always quite a challenge."

It was nothing like the challenge the Giants faced from Wainwright, who had lasted just $2^{1}/_{3}$ innings in his previous postseason start. A mix of biting curveballs and well placed cutters left the Giants shaking their heads, and more often than not, making a short jog back to the visitor's dugout.

"I think Wainwright today was as good as you're going to see," Pence said. "He was spot on with his location. Some days you get your hits, and some days you're just a click off."

The Giants have been a couple clicks off in St. Louis.

After his team left 11 runners on base in Game 3, manager Bruce Bochy moved Buster Posey up to the No. 3 spot for the second time this year and dropped Sandoval to the cleanup spot. Sanchez caught Lincecum, bumping Brandon Belt to the bench.

The new look wasn't any better than the old one.

Wainwright gave up four hits in seven innings and needed just 96 pitches to cruise through the Giants' lineup.

"He had us off balance," left fielder Gregor Blanco said. "He was mixing all his pitches, throwing strikes. He was really good."

The Giants haven't been, especially in the heart of the order. Posey is 2 for 14 in the NLCS, Sandoval is 4 for 17 and Pence is 2 for 15. Sanchez hit fifth Thursday but couldn't provide a spark, going 0 for 4 with three strikeouts.

"Baseball isn't always easy," Pence said. "Sometimes pitchers are going to beat you."

For the Giants, there has been no "sometimes" with Barry Zito on the mound. They have won the last 12 times Zito, the Game 5 starter, has taken the mound, a streak that started Aug. 7 in St. Louis.

"Zito has been tremendous for us," Pence said. "We've got to find a way to get a win tomorrow, and if we go home to (Ryan) Vogelsong and (Matt) Cain throwing, we'll feel pretty good."

Pence led the charge the first time the Giants' backs touched up against the wall, giving inspirational pregame speeches that sparked a comeback against the Reds. He has no plans to morph into Reverend Pence before Game 5.

"Everyone is aware of our situation," he said. ■

Tim Lincecum sits on the bench in the fifth inning. In his only postseason start in 2012, the former Cy Young Award winner allowed four earned runs in $4^{2}/_{3}$ innings as the Cardinals moved within one game of the World Series. (Nhat V. Meyer/Staff)

NATIONAL LEAGUE CHAMPIONSHIP SERIES: GAME 5
OCTOBER 19, 2012 | GIANTS 5, CARDINALS 0

Bring It All Back Home

Zito Is Superb as S.F. Staves Off Elimination

By Alex Pavlovic

> **I'm known for my Arabian horse gallop. I'm just not that fast. To bunt for a hit you've got to be perfect, and fortunately it was."**
>
> — **Pitcher Barry Zito**

ST. LOUIS—Facing elimination for the fourth time in 11 days, the Giants scripted a new motto: "Do everything you can to get home."

Thanks to Barry Zito, who contributed on the mound and at the plate, the Giants are going back to AT&T Park, and not just to pack up their belongings. Zito was spectacular Friday in a 5-0 victory over the St. Louis Cardinals that cut the Cardinals' lead in the National League Championship Series to 3-2.

"That was the goal coming in," said shortstop Brandon Crawford, who had a two-run single. "We wanted to get this series home and play another day together."

Zito clinched that goal with a performance he called the biggest of his career.

The left-hander pitched $7^2/_3$ shutout innings in his most important start as a Giant, weathering an early storm to give the lineup a chance to jump on Cardinals right-hander Lance Lynn.

The Giants scored four runs in the fourth inning to improve to 4-0 in elimination games. For the fourth time, there was a fiery speech, but this time Hunter Pence wasn't the only one playing the part of reverend. Several players stood up and urged the team to get the series back to San Francisco, where the Giants will start Ryan Vogelsong in Sunday's Game 6 and have Matt Cain waiting for a potential Game 7.

"They're our guys, and they're two of the best in the game," Pence said. "We're

Pablo Sandoval welcomes Hunter Pence home after both runners scored on Brandon Crawford's fourth-inning RBI single. (Nhat V. Meyer/Staff)

"Everyone counted us out four or five times this year already. It's not over until the last out is made." — Pitcher Ryan Vogelsong

excited. Our backs are against the wall again, but we're not going to fold."

Nobody would have blamed Zito if he folded long ago. He hasn't lived up to a massive $126 million contract and was left off the 2010 postseason roster, but Zito never stopped eyeing a potential moment of redemption. Teammates laud Zito for his work ethic and ability to bounce back from rough stretches, of which there have been many.

On Friday, it was mostly smooth sailing.

Zito escaped an early jam when he got Lynn to hit into an inning-ending double play with the bases loaded in the second.

"We're hoping he'd either hit a fly ball deep or swing and miss," Cardinals manager Mike Matheny said.

Lynn did neither, and the Giants took a collective sigh of relief.

"That gave us a little momentum," Crawford said. "Zito being able to pitch out of that was huge for us, and we were able to come back two innings later."

The fourth-inning four-spot started with singles from Marco Scutaro and Pablo Sandoval. With one out, Pence hit a chopper to the mound that looked like the start of a double play, but Lynn fired the ball off second base and into center field, allowing Scutaro to score.

As Pence stood on first base, Roberto Kelly, coaching first base for the first time since getting hit by a line drive last Saturday, leaned over.

"He said, 'That's the break we need,'" Pence said.

Crawford provided the back-breaker with the latest in a series of clutch hits for a young shortstop with a habit of coming through in big spots. Crawford scorched a run-scoring triple to get the Giants on the board in Game 5 of the NLDS; this time it was just a well-placed ground ball up the middle on a 3-2 pitch with the bases loaded that brought two runs home.

"Lynn needed to throw a strike," Crawford said. "He

didn't have anywhere else to put me."

The position players have talked all postseason about getting a big early lead for their starters, but on this night they didn't feel that Zito needed much help.

"One run probably would have been enough with Zito pitching the way he did," Crawford said.

Zito felt otherwise, and on a night when he surprised nearly everyone outside the Giants clubhouse with his magnificent pitching, Zito surprised even his own manager with a perfect bunt down the third base line that scored Gregor Blanco and gave the Giants a 4-0 lead.

It was Zito's first career postseason hit and RBI, and the first bunt single of his entire career.

"I'm known for my Arabian horse gallop," Zito said, smiling. "I'm just not that fast. To bunt for a hit you've got to be perfect, and fortunately it was."

There was nothing lucky about the rest of Zito's night. He kept the Cardinals off balance, retiring 15 of 16 starting with Lynn's double-play grounder to short. When Daniel Descalso threatened to start a rally with a two-out single in the seventh, Zito threw an 85 mph fastball past Pete Kozma to get out of the inning.

Zito became the first Giants starter this postseason to come out for the eighth inning and was removed after two outs as the infielders ran to the mound to pat him on the chest. Zito gave up six hits, walked one, struck out six and threw 115 pitches, his most since Aug. 6, 2010, a span of 80 starts.

"I couldn't be happier for him," manager Bruce Bochy said. "He put on quite a show."

The win was the Giants' 13th straight in a game started by Zito and guaranteed a fifth elimination game for a team that looks very relaxed when backs are against the wall.

"Everyone counted us out four or five times this year already," said Vogelsong, the Game 6 starter. "It's not over until the last out is made." ∎

In his most important performance in a Giants uniform, Barry Zito pitched 7²/₃ scoreless innings, leading the Giants to a 5-0 win and sending the series back to San Francisco. (Karl Mondon/Staff)

NATIONAL LEAGUE CHAMPIONSHIP SERIES: GAME 6
OCTOBER 21, 2012 | GIANTS 6, CARDINALS 1

Here Comes Seventh Heaven

Vogelsong Sets the Tone Early

By Alex Pavlovic

We're one win away from the World Series, and we know what kind of a feeling it was before. We want that feeling again.

— Closer Sergio Romo

SAN FRANCISCO—After dominating in the first two postseason starts of his long career, Ryan Vogelsong said it was too early to say he was a big-game pitcher.

How about now?

Vogelsong was unhittable for much of a 6-1 victory over the St. Louis Cardinals at AT&T Park that sent the National League Championship Series to a winner-take-all Game 7. The right-hander struck out a career-high nine and took a no-hitter into the fifth inning while giving up a lone run for the third time in three postseason starts.

"It feels great," Vogelsong said. "I didn't want to let these guys down. I didn't want to let the city down."

Instead, Vogelsong moved the Giants and San Francisco within one victory of another round of World Series baseball. The victory was the fifth straight in an elimination game for the Giants, who send Matt Cain to the mound against the Cardinals' Kyle Lohse in Monday's Game 7.

"We're one win away from the World Series, and we know what kind of a feeling it was before," closer Sergio Romo said. "We want that feeling again. Imagine if we can do it again."

Vogelsong has been picturing this moment his whole life, and he's not the only one. Marco Scutaro, who again paced the lineup, is on the verge of his first World Series.

"For me, that's priceless," he said.

Scutaro was sitting on a podium next

Giants starter Ryan Vogelsong took a no-hitter into the fifth inning and struck out nine as the Giants topped the Cardinals 6-1 to force a deciding Game 7 of the National League Championship Series. (Nhat V. Meyer/Staff)

to Vogelsong, who wore a content look on his face as he soaked in the aftermath of his latest clutch showing as a Giant. Vogelsong is 2-0 in the series and has given up just two runs in 14 innings. Through three starts this postseason, Vogelsong has given up 11 hits and three runs in 19 innings while striking out 18.

The dominance started early Sunday. Vogelsong fired fastballs on his first 13 pitches as a sellout crowd reached a deafening level and teammates watched in amazement. Vogelsong struck out three in the first inning while throwing fastballs on 16 of 18 pitches and often hitting 94 mph.

"We were on the same page with that one," catcher Buster Posey said of the fastball flood. "It seems his velocity has been a little higher the last five or six starts. It was electric, no doubt about it."

Vogelsong didn't allow a hit until the fifth, when Daniel Descalso and Pete Kozma singled with two outs. He didn't allow a run until the sixth, when Allen Craig's two-out single scored Carlos Beltran, who had doubled.

"He did everything he wanted to do to us," Cardinals manager Mike Matheny said. "He's made some great pitches against us, and we've made very little adjustments."

The Giants, with help from the Cardinals' shaky defense, gave Vogelsong a big early lead. Scutaro walked with one out in the first, advanced on Pablo Sandoval's double, and scored on a ground out by Posey.

Brandon Belt led off the second with a triple. The Cardinals intentionally walked Brandon Crawford two batters later to get to Vogelsong, but Kozma couldn't make the play when Vogelsong pulled back a bunt attempt and slashed a chopper to short. Belt scored as Vogelsong reached first base safely.

The Cardinals have allowed multiple unearned runs in all three of their losses and have given up an NLCS record 10 unearned runs through six games.

"You try and put as much pressure on them as possible," Belt said. "You put runners on base and push,

and stuff like this happens. We're doing the same thing we've been doing all season: Find some way to get on base, some way to get into scoring position and then some way to get home."

Scutaro hit a double two batters later, scoring Crawford and Vogelsong. The second baseman is 9 for 19 since nearly being knocked out of the series on a hard Matt Holliday slide in Game 2.

"I think a lot of the nation is finally getting to see the player that Marco is," Vogelsong said. "The things that he's doing aren't surprising to anybody on this club."

Facing elimination in Game 5, the Giants had a four-run rally that included three singles, an error, a walk and a bunt hit by Barry Zito. The four-run Game 6 rally was built around a single, double, triple, intentional walk and error.

"You can't try and hit a 20-run homer," Angel Pagan said. "We're going out there to score runs and win games, and it doesn't matter how it happens."

The Giants don't care how they win Game 7, either. They'll send Cain, who gave up three runs in 6²/₃ innings in Game 3, up against Lohse, who gave up seven hits and walked five that night but allowed just one run in a 3-1 Cardinals victory.

After becoming the third team in history to win a fifth elimination game, the Giants feel comfortable in this position. The Cardinals do, too. The last Game 7 in the NLCS was in 2006, when the Cardinals rallied for a win after losing Game 6 on the road to the New York Mets.

"You could have probably predicted this before the series," Belt said. "Neither team gives up. Tomorrow we'll both scrap."

After scratching and clawing their way back into a second straight series, the Giants were all smiles while talking about the coming Game 7. The consensus in the clubhouse was that the biggest concern Sunday night was simply finding a way to get some sleep.

"This is special," Posey said. "It doesn't get much better than this." ∎

Marco Scutaro hits a two-run RBI double in the second inning. Scutaro was 2-for-3 in the win. (Nhat V. Meyer/Staff)

NATIONAL LEAGUE CHAMPIONSHIP SERIES: GAME 7
OCTOBER 22, 2012 | GIANTS 9, CARDINALS 0

Bring On Detroit

Giants Return to World Series, Romp in Rainy Clincher

By Alex Pavlovic

> It was surreal. It never rains like that here. That was the perfect amount of drama on top of drama. The night ended magically."
>
> — Pitcher Barry Zito

SAN FRANCISCO—The comeback kings will play for baseball's greatest crown.

The Giants blew past the St. Louis Cardinals on Monday at AT&T Park, winning 9-0 in Game 7 of the National League Championship Series to complete a second straight historic comeback and advance to the World Series for the second time in three seasons. The Giants are the first team in MLB history to win six elimination games en route to the World Series.

"It's hard to comprehend," catcher Buster Posey said. "When your backs are against the wall, you just play for that game. You have to believe you have a great group of guys that can do this, and we do.

"We never got ahead of ourselves, and this is the result."

The coming result is Wednesday's Game 1 of the World Series at AT&T Park against the Detroit Tigers. The immediate result was a scene Giants fans will never forget.

The Giants roared to victory behind the predictable and the unbelievable. Matt Cain shut the Cardinals out for $5^2/_3$ gutty innings, and series MVP Marco Scutaro went 3 for 4 to tie an LCS record with 14 hits in a series. But the game turned on Hunter Pence's two-run double that appeared to literally turn in midair.

"The baseball gods helped us with that ball," manager Bruce Bochy said.

The baseball gods conspired with Mother Nature to set a dramatic scene as this historic set of Giants put a twist on the age-old tradition of soaking each other with champagne. This time, the Giants got soaked before the victory was official.

The skies opened up in the ninth inning as puddles formed around the infield and groundskeepers rushed to rebuild a

Marco Scutaro (left) lets out a yell as he and Buster Posey score on a Hunter Pence double in the third inning. The Giants, once within a game of elimination, led the deciding game 7-0 after three innings. (Nhat V. Meyer/Staff)

"We just got a lot of momentum going our way. It started with (Barry) Zito." — Pitcher Matt Cain

mound that Sergio Romo would take for the final out.

As a deafening crowd cheered, Romo got a fitting final out. Five games after nearly knocking Scutaro out of the series with a hard slide at second base, Matt Holliday popped out to the second baseman.

"It was surreal," said pitcher Barry Zito, who turned the momentum with 7 2/3 shutout innings in Game 5. "It never rains like that here. That was the perfect amount of drama on top of drama. The night ended magically."

After overcoming a 2-0 deficit to the Cincinnati Reds to advance out of the NLDS, the Giants fell behind 3-1 to the Cardinals. Zito put the team on his back in Game 5, followed by Ryan Vogelsong in Game 6 and Cain in Game 7. In the final three games, the Giants outscored the dangerous Cardinals 20-1.

"We just got a lot of momentum going our way," Cain said. "It started with Zito."

Actually, it started at the trade deadline. The Giants went out and dealt for Pence, the emotional leader of this postseason run, and Scutaro, who hit .500 in the NLCS. Both players were heavily involved Monday.

The Giants led 2-0 heading into the third inning and promptly knocked Cardinals starter Kyle Lohse out of the game with a Scutaro single, Pablo Sandoval double and Posey walk that loaded the bases. Joe Kelly entered to face Pence, who has sparked the comebacks with fiery speeches but entered Game 7 with just one postseason RBI.

On Pence's first day after being traded to San Francisco from the Philadelphia Phillies, the right fielder smiled and warned reporters, "I have to be honest, every now and then, I do things you don't see very often." That turned out to be the understatement of the season.

Pence broke his bat on a 95 mph fastball but the ball hit the bat three times, once at contact and twice as Pence followed through with a shattered bat. The result was a knuckleball to shortstop, and Pete Kozma initially broke to his right before unsuccessfully sprawling back to his left as the ball shot into the outfield.

Scutaro and Sandoval scored easily, and Posey, who couldn't even run when spring training began, sprinted home when Jon Jay overran the ball in center.

"It was weird — but I was happy," Pence said. "I've had a lot of weird broken-bat hits, but that ranks up there. You know, it's baseball, you can't explain it even if you play."

That's as good an explanation as any for Scutaro's resurgence. The 36-year-old was picked up at the deadline because the Giants needed a fill-in for Sandoval, who was injured. Scutaro helped the lineup become a grind-it-out powerhouse, and in this series became the first player in LCS history to have six multi-hit games.

"To live this experience for me is unbelievable," Scutaro said. "I've played with a bunch of guys with a span of years in the big leagues that never had the opportunity to be in the playoffs or play in the World Series. Now I'm going."

Scutaro was a rock throughout the series and again on Monday night, when the Cardinals inexplicably fell apart. A mental mistake and another fielding mistake by Kozma opened the floodgates far before the rain came. By the time the third inning was over, the Giants had a 7-0 lead.

"It all happened really quickly," Posey said.

The entire comeback did, just as it had in the previous round.

"Hey, it's baseball," Romo said, smiling wide and soaked in rain and champagne. "You never quite know what you're going to get." ∎

Matt Cain pitched 5 2/3 scoreless innings as the Giants advanced to their second World Series in three seasons. (Gary Reyes/Staff)

Giants (from left) Brandon Crawford, Angel Pagan, Marco Scutaro and Hunter Pence celebrate after the final out of Game 7 as the Giants captured the National League pennant. (Nhat V. Meyer/Staff)